James H. Scates

The Divine Origin and Authority of the Bible

James H. Scates

The Divine Origin and Authority of the Bible

ISBN/EAN: 9783337171582

Printed in Europe, USA, Canada, Australia, Japan

Cover: Foto ©Lupo / pixelio.de

More available books at **www.hansebooks.com**

THE DIVINE ORIGIN

—AND—

AUTHORITY OF THE BIBLE.

ESTABLISHED FROM A NEW TRAIN OF
FACTS AND ARGUMENTS.

DESIGNED FOR

THE COMFORT OF CHRISTIANS AND THE CONVICTION OF UNBELIEVERS.

BY

REV. JAMES H. SCATES,
Center, Texas.

LOUISVILLE, KY.:
BAPTIST BOOK CONCERN,
1896.

PREFACE.

Believing that a small work, setting forth in simple language some of the evidences of the divine origin and authority of the Bible would be acceptable to the masses of the people and would be read with interest and profit by them, I have written the present work. It is not a compilation, but almost an exclusively original composition, presenting new arguments and evidences not to be found elsewhere. Vast efforts are being made by professed scientists and infidels to undermine the Bible, and thus overthrow the Christian faith. But all their efforts will prove futile and vain. They will only pull down destruction upon themselves, while the Book will stand, as it has always stood, all the wrath of men and the malice of devils. You must not suppose that this is all that can be said in defense of the Bible. It is a very meager sketch. *It is not the thousandth part.* Volumes upon volumes might be written without exhausting it. Evidences of Christianity have been written oftentimes by profoundly able and scholarly men, but THE EVIDENCES (that is all the evidences) have never been written, and never can be written, for they sweep the universe.

DEDICATION.

To the people of the living God is this book affectionately dedicated. May it confirm their faith, brighten their hopes, animate their zeal, assuage their sorrows, and cheer them in their conflict with sin, and earth, and hell.

CHAPTER I.

THE EXISTENCE OF GOD.

THE religious feeling is the most pervading and powerful of the human heart. Wherever man has been found his leading and distinguishing characteristic has been that he was a worshipping creature. It is certain that he will worship something,—sun, moon, stars, stocks, stones, beast of the field, or some other object. So strong is this feeling implanted in his nature that it has often led him to the sacrifice of his own offspring to propitiate his offended deities.

Now what does this undeniable fact prove?

Why, that there is somewhere an object of worship—that there is somewhere a Supreme Intelligence to whom is due the adoration of the human heart. The possession of sight implies the existence of light, otherwise sight is useless. Hence, fishes in dark caves lose their sense of seeing. The possession of hearing implies the existence of sound; of smell the existence of odors. So we see there is a correspondence between all the senses and the objects that call them forth and bring them into exercise. So of man's mental faculties. On every hand he is surrounded by the profoundest problems demanding his investigation and solution. Without this mental discipline, he could never be strengthened and developed. In like manner in regard to man's moral and spiritual nature. There is no faculty of the human mind or affection of the human heart without a corresponding object to call forth its exercise and to satisfy its wants. Thus we see there is an absolute correlation existing throughout the whole creation—wants on the one hand, and objects to gratify those wants on the other. Now the point of the argument is this: as we have light for the eye, sound for the ear, odor for the nostrils, and problems for the mind; so we must have God for the worshipping faculty. If we have not, then there is a break in the unity and harmony of the laws of nature. There is a link out of the chain that throws the whole order of the universe into confusion.

Now there is another strange fact in the history of our race. And that is the universal sense of sin. Amongst all people in every stage of civilization, under every form of government, through all ages, this has been true. How will you account for this undeniable fact? It can only be done by admitting the existence of a *Supreme Being* whose laws man has transgressed. These laws were originally inscribed upon man's heart. They were incorporated into his very constitution; and tho' blurred and dimmed their power is still felt by every human being, always testifying to the existence of law and a *Lawgiver*.

Again, let us walk forth some calm, clear, beautiful night and lift our eyes to the starry canopy and behold the millions and millions of flaming orbs in the heavens, rolling in grandeur and magnificence through the fields of space, burning suns, fiery comets, blazing meteors. I ask how came they there? Who made them?

To this question but one answer can be given. That answer is, Almighty God—Omnipotent, Omniscient, Eternal. Look out upon the broad ocean. See those mighty ships plowing the briny deep! Does any one doubt that some one made them? None. Neither can we doubt when we behold the great worlds moving in grandeur and glory some one made them, even God. If one is a legitimate inference so is the other. If you accept one you cannot reject the other.

Observe likewise the beauty, harmony and design displayed in their construction and movements. How came all this? Where there is design and adaptation there must be intelligence. These must find their basis in God.

The deepest intuitions of reason and the human heart in all ages and amongst all nations have instinctively acknowledged the same great truth—the existence of a Supreme Power. Perhaps ten thousand to one of all the multitudes of earth have accepted this fact. It may not be within the range of the human mind to originate the idea of God; but being once revealed, it can never be lost; because it falls in with and meets the wants of his nature and is the key to the mysteries of his being and the wonders of the universe.

When we turn to man's moral and spiritual nature, we are involved in utter bewilderment unless we accept the existence of a Supreme Being. Here is a wild waste wrapped in gloom and hopeless darkness, if there be no God. No genius, no learning, no talent can penetrate the inextricable maze—night broods over the profound deep. Whence did that strange faculty called *conscience* come?—conscience that takes cognizance of the moral qualities of actions—approves the right and condemns the wrong. But there can be no right and wrong unless there is a *law* determining it. And there can be no law without a Lawgiver, who is the everlasting Creator and Preserver of all things.

It is an established and certain fact that all life is derived. There can be no life without antecedent life. There can be no self-originating life. This being so, it is demonstrably certain that all the life in the world must have come down from the great center and source of all life, that is from God.

To recapitulate briefly the argument:

I have shown the existence of God—

First—From the worshipping faculty in man which necessarily involves the idea of God, the object to be worshipped.

Second—I have shown the existence of God from the universal sense of sin which involves the existence of violated law—law necessarily implies a Lawgiver—that is God.

Third—I have shown that the whole material universe testifies to the existence of God, both in its magnitude and design.

Fourth—I have shown that it was almost the universal sentiment of the race that some being made and governed the world.

Fifth—I have shown from conscience that notes the difference between right and wrong, that no such thing as right and wrong could exist without a Supreme Power to establish that difference.

Sixth—I showed that all life is derived—no life is self-originating. This is the clearest deductions of science. Hence all the life in the world must have come down from the great source and fountain of all life, that is from God.

These evidences might be multiplied almost indefinitely, but it does not comport with my design to elaborate any subject, but merely to sketch the outlines of truth.

CHAPTER II.

GOD BEING BENEVOLENT, MUST NECESSARILY HAVE MADE A REVELATION TO MAN; THE BIBLE MUST BE THAT REVELATION, AS IT SOLVES ALL THE GREAT PROBLEMS THAT CONFRONT US, SUCH AS THE ORIGIN OF THE UNIVERSE, THE ENTRANCE OF MAN ON THIS SPHERE, THE BEGINNING OF LIFE, THE ORIGIN OF MORAL SIN.

NOW it is manifest that this being, whose existence we have proven, is a being of infinite power and wisdom. That he is likewise benevolent is evident from the fact that the pleasures of life vastly outweigh the miseries, and that the most bountiful provision has been made on every hand for man's development, comfort and happiness.

It is further clear that in the whole creation, there was nothing made with the design of causing suffering—that is, suffering was not the primary design of its creation; suffering being merely incidental and the sequence of violated law. It was introduced into the system to remind man of his dependence and mortality, and to keep perpetually before his mind the mournful fact that he was a transgressor of God's holy law.

Now, if God be benevolent, he certainly would not have left his creature, man, without any knowledge of his origin, duty and destiny; how he came into this world; the relations he sustains to his Creator; the duties he owes to him and to his fellow-man. He likewise would certainly have given him a knowledge of the creation of the world and all things, seeing it was an utter impossibility for him to have learned these things in any other way than by a direct revelation.

This being premised, it follows that any book from God must give an account of the origin of the universe; for evidently the world was made before man was placed upon it. Hence, the world being created before man was, it was impossible for the latter to know how the former came into being unless God made it known to him. Therefore, if we have any knowledge whatever of the beginning of the material universe it must have come to us by revelation.

Now, in the Bible we have a plain, simple statement of the origin of things. It says, "In the beginning God created the heavens and the earth." Here is no speculation, no conjecture, no theorizing; but a plain statement of fact. How strongly this narrative contrasts with all other accounts of creation. This is the only plausible or rational account that has ever been given, or can be given. Outside of this all is conjecture, assumption, surmising. We must, then, accept the Bible statement in regard to this matter, or remain forever in hopeless darkness on this subject. For independent of this account there is not one single gleam of light to illumine our pathway. We must walk by this light or walk in darkness the balance of our days. The learned have never been able to frame even a plausible theory on this question —one that is supported by even a solitary fact.

There is another problem that has puzzled the inquiries of all ages, and that is, how man became an inhabitant of this globe. That he is here is an undoubted fact. How did he come here? The Bible says, "God created him out of the dust of the earth." The scientist says, he was evolved through countless ages from a moneron, or monad, the lowest order of animated life—a mere speck of jelly-like substance—and passed on by successive steps through all the grades of animated nature—fish, reptile, monkey, etc., up to man. This is pure assumption, unsupported by any facts whatever. Moreover, it involves a complete change in the laws of nature, for the race is not multiplied in this way now.

In this connection, we will call your attention to another grave question with which the learned world have grappled in vain, and that is, the origin of life. Now, what life is in its essence, no man living knows. Science can not even give a definition of it. We only know it by its manifestations. But that it is something, a reality, a substantial entity, is undeniable. *There was a time when there was no life on this globe.* This is agreed on all hands. This is alike the teaching of the Bible and the most advanced science. Geologists point us to the primary strata of the earth and show that they contain no organic remains whatever. Again, they point us to the higher strata, and show us imbedded in the solid rock myriads of once living creatures. Life suddenly appears. Whence did it come? The Bible says it came from God—God created the fowls of the air, the fish of the sea and the beasts of the field. And of man it is said, "God breathed into his nostrils the breath of life; and man became a living soul." Now, we must accept this account, or admit that life rose spontaneously, that is, without a cause. To do this is to ignore all the experience of the race, the facts of science and the dictates of reason. Hence we see that whenever we leave the Bible we are at once surrounded on all sides by inextricable difficulties—by questions it is impossible for the human intellect ever to solve. The mightiest minds of earth stand absolutely appalled and helpless when brought to face the questions we have been so briefly considering.

There is no possible solution of them but that which the Bible gives. This we must accept, or, like the little caged bird, we must beat the bars of our prison house through never ending years.

But we are not yet through the discussion of these primary problems, which have so much interested inquirers in all ages. The next we present is the origin of moral evil. This is the mystery of mysteries. Prodigious efforts through long ages have been made to account for it.

The mightiest intellects of earth have wrestled in vain with it. Like the stone of Sysiphus it has always rolled back into the awful depths of its own profundity. They have been utterly confounded and bewildered when they have attempted to account for it. That it is here is a mournful fact. Its shadow is upon every heart, its blight upon every life. I ask whence did it come? How did it happen that a curse so withering entered this fair and beautiful world? I ask the wise men of the world. I ask the hoary headed sage. I ask the philosophy of all ages! All dumb—all silent as the grave. No response comes to the inquiry. In sadness and sorrow I turn my thoughts within and ask my soul: O why am I so far off from God and holiness? So estranged from good? So prone to evil? No answer comes up from the deep depths of my heart. I turn to the Bible. It is all radiant with light. It is all aglow with life. It tells me God made man upright—endowed him with ability to stand, tho' free to fall. He placed him in a garden of delights, all beautiful and glorious. He walked in fellowship with his Creator, and held sweet communion with God; but in an hour of temptation he transgressed the divine law, lost his allegiance to his Maker, and thus introduced death into the world and "all our woe." Since which misery has followed his footsteps—his life is a life of unrest—a life of toil and sorrow till death cuts him down and the grave swallows him up. Such is the Bible account of the entrance of sin into the world. Now what shall we do about it? Shall we accept the light or remain in hopeless ignorance on the subject forever? Unaided by divine revelation man has never been able to offer anything whatever in solution of this problem. Without this, there is no star in the horizon to shine upon our pathway—no light to illumine the darkness that surrounds us. Shall we walk by the light we have, or shall we grope our way in the gloom of night? For my part, I accept the light and rejoice in it.

There is another fact that has an important bearing in this connection and which furnishes the most convincing proof of the divine origin of the Bible. That fact is the curse which we are told God pronounced on the earth for man's sake—that thorns and thistles should it bring forth. Now here is a curse pronounced thousands of years ago, the fulfillment of which lies right before our eyes. It is a matter of daily realization by the whole race through all ages. Now how was it possible for any one to know that this curse would hold good through all time, but God or he to whom God should reveal it? It is not natural nor possible for the ground itself to discriminate against cereals and in favor of noxious weeds. Why is it that one grows spontaneously and the other only under diligent culture? They require the same soil—the same light and heat—the same moisture. I ask the botanist, I ask the scientist, Why the difference? No answer can be given but the Bible answer—the earth still groans under the primeval curse. Here then is a great fact recorded ages ago in the Bible, testified by all history and verified by every man's daily experience. What will you do with it? You can not deny it. You must accept it. If you accept it, you accept the Bible as the Book of God.

Before concluding this chapter there is one more question of vital importance to which I invite your attention; and that is the curse of labor. Why is it that man, the noblest of God's creatures, is doomed to perpetual toil—toil, toil for a bare subsistence—exposed to the summer's sun and the winter's storm. The birds of the air and the beasts of the field are furnished with natural clothing for their protection and food for their sustenance. But man, poor man, must labor and dig and delve for a support. Why this? We must go back to the Bible for an answer. Human learning utterly fails to meet the inquiry. It has absolutely nothing to say on the question. The Bible statement is, "In the sweat of thy face shalt thou eat bread, till thou return unto the ground." This was because man had sinned.

CHAPTER III.

MIRACLES.

THE Bible furthermore gives us an account of the Israelites, the most peculiar and wonderful people that ever lived. Their history is absolutely unparalleled. It tells of the call of Abraham, their ancestor; of God's covenant with him and his promise to make a great nation of his posterity; of his son Isaac and the renewal of the promise to him; and likewise of his offspring, Esau and Jacob. It tells how the latter after a train of providential events moved down into Egypt and there by a strange mutation of fortune became bondsman to the Egyptians. It gives us an account of Moses and his wonderful preservation; of his call to be their leader and deliverer. It tell us of the wonderful miracles Moses wrought before Pharaoh in order to induce him to let the people go; such as turning the waters of the Nile into blood; covering the land with frogs, lice, flies; afflicting cattle with murrain, the people with boils; calling up myriads of locusts; covering the land with darkness and causing the death of the firstborn in every Egyptian family.

Now it must be confessed that these were very extraordinary events. If Moses actually performed these wonders they stamp him as commissioned from God. Now let us briefly examine these miracles and see whether or not they are supported by adequate testimony. If they are, then the divine mission of Moses and the claims of the Old Testament to be the word of God are fully authenticated. If they are not, we need not prosecute our inquiries any farther; for if we fail here in these fundamental facts, we fail all along the line. What evidence, then, have we that these miracles were really wrought? I answer, the evidence of the whole Jewish nation, some three millions of people, who were present and were eyewitnesses of their occurrence. You say they were mistaken. This is utterly inadmissible. These miracles were too marvellous, too diversified, too long continued, too public and notorious to admit of any such supposition. If people cannot believe the evidences of their senses—what they see, hear and feel—what can they believe? But you do not escape the difficulty by claiming that they were mistaken, if such were the case. You only avoid one difficulty by encountering a greater; and that is, three millions of people believed they saw the waters of the Nile turned into blood when they saw no such thing; that three millions of people believed they saw myriads of locusts devouring every green thing when there was not a locust in all the land; that three millions of people believed they heard the wail of sorrow in every Egyptian family because of the death of the firstborn when no body at all had died. Furthermore, that three millions of people believed they were delivered from the most abject slavery; led out by a high hand; passed dry shod through the Red sea; were guided by a pillar of cloud by day and a pillar of fire by night; were fed by manna and quails, drank water from the smitten rock and all this through a space of forty years; and finally crossed the Jordan, which parted its waters for this purpose, and entered triumphantly into the land of Canaan. If they were deceived in regard to the miracles wrought in Egypt for their deliverance, they must have been deceived in regard to all those accompanying their march through the wilderness and their entrance into the promised land. If they were mistaken, then you have on your hands a miracle vastly transcending all the others put together. You must account for the fact that the Jews believed all these things. They believed them because they witnessed them, because they had personal knowledge of their reality. They could not have been deceived in regard to them. There is no room for any supposition. It is utterly absurd. They could not be deceived in regard to the most pal-

AUTHORITY OF THE BIBLE.   23

pable facts of which the senses can take cognizance. We are then absolutely shut up to the belief that these events took place. If they did, they show beyond all controversy the divine origin of the Bible. We see then that the claims of the Bible to be from heaven do not rest upon tradition, or educational bias, or mere assumptions, but upon the most substantial facts addressed to our reason and sober judgment.

But this is not all the evidence we have. It has been the custom of all ages and nations to perpetuate great national events by the observance of a day, the erection of monuments, or the keeping of festivals. Thus in our history the observance of the Fourth of July keeps in remembrance the fact that the Declaration of Independence took place on that day.

In Boston, there is a vast granite pile called Bunker Hill Monument, built to keep in remembrance the fact that a great battle was fought there. Likewise in Baltimore there is the Washington Monument, erected to perpetuate the character and services of the Father of his Country. So our government is now engaged in setting apart and marking with statues and monuments the locality of great battles in the late war.

Now we read in the Bible that the very night of the departure of the Israelites from Egypt the angel of the Lord swept through the land

and laid low in death the firstborn of every Egyptian family, sparing the firstborn of every Hebrew family. This remarkable event must have deeply and profoundly impressed every heart, both of the Egyptians and the Hebrews. Now that it might never be forgotten, that it might be kept in perpetual remembrance through all generations, God directed that a feast called the Passover should be instituted. It was called the Passover because the angel of death in his flight thro' the land passed over all those houses on whose lintels and doorposts was found sprinkled the blood of the paschal lamb. Now it is notorious and undeniable that this feast originating under such circumstances and appointed for such a purpose has been continued by the Jews through all ages down to the present time so far as has been practicable in their dispersed condition. Now let me ask, "Does the observance of the 4th of July by the American people prove that the Declaration of Independence took place on that day?" You answer, yes. If so, does not the observance of the Passover prove that the firstborn of every Egyptian family was slain on the night of the departure of the Israelites? You must answer, yes. If one is demonstrative evidence, so is the other; for they are exactly parallel. If you accept the one you must accept the other. No possible reply can be made to this argument.

Nor is this all. There was the feast of Pentecost, observed in commemoration of the giving of the law on Mt. Sinai. The people were to be reminded of their bondage in Egypt, and they were especially admonished of their obligation to keep the divine commandments. (Deut.16:12.)

FEAST OF TABERNACLES.

The Jews, in migrating from Egypt into Canaan, dwelt in booths, or tents. To keep fresh in their memory the great facts of their deliverance and journey through the wilderness the Feast of Tabernacles was appointed. When the feast fell on a Sabbatical year, portions of the Law were read each day to men, women, children and strangers. (Deut. 31:10-13.) In this feast their journeyings were portrayed, and thus vividly kept in remembrance. They were, in point of fact, enacted over in miniature. The great events of their deliverance from bondage, the giving of the Law and their journeyings were thus interwoven into the very fabric of their institutions, and have been continued down to the present time. Did it comport with the design of this work, we should like to elaborate more fully this subject and bring out in full force the tremendous evidence that is in it. Suffice it to say, no other people, either in ancient or modern times, can present *one-hundredth part* of the testimony to the facts of their history that the Jews can. The history of all other people is shrouded in darkness and doubt more or less, especially in their earlier periods. The facts recorded are rather conjectural than otherwise—no competent witnesses having ever observed and reported them, and no memorials having ever been erected to perpetuate them. Now, here to-day, right before our eyes, *in our very midst*, is this wonderful people who can trace back their history to the remotest antiquity—to their very first progenitor, Abraham. These people were personally cognizant of all the great events of their history; these events were recorded by their leader and lawgiver at the time of their occurrence, read in their hearing and received their sanction. They were likewise embodied in memorial observances which have come down to the present time.

Besides these, there were many other feasts among the Jews—all referring back in some way to the facts of their deliverance, and at the same time pointing forward to man's spiritual deliverance from the thraldom of sin through the sacrifice and mediation of Christ. In fact, no writings in the world are so rich in original and primitive ideas and fundamental principles. Never in the history of the earth is there to be found a system so peculiar, so wonderful, so unapproachable. Man, unaided by revelation, could no more have devised it than he could have created the world. After the study of thousands of years we are just beginning to understand its marvellous depths and amazing riches.

Another very striking and conclusive proof of the divine origin of the Old Testament is derived from the burdensome character of the Jewish religion. It is a well-known fact that the Jews are the most money-loving and money-getting people in the world. Now, this people, it is estimated, gave one-half of all their income (counting their time) to support their religion. This they certainly would not have done unless it had been attested by the most overwhelming proofs of its divine origin. That their religion was from heaven was to their minds the most certain of all truths. The writers claimed to have received their knowledge from God. This of itself is a very strong proof when we consider their modesty and humility, the dignity of their character and the moral excellence of their lives.

There is another provision in the Mosaic Institutions that render it positively certain that those institutions were of divine origin. I allude to that requirement of the law that forbid the sowing of the land every seventh year—the land was to rest. Now, no mere human legislator would ever have ventured to insert such a provision in his code unless he had received express instructions from God; because without *God's providential care* such an enactment would have resulted in famine and ruin. It would do it now. No people can afford to withhold sowing without meeting dire calamity. But the Jews did this, not only every seventh year, but likewise every year of Jubilee. And did it without detriment, because God made provision for their support.

There is still another very remarkable provision in the Mosaic laws which stamp those laws with divine origin and authority. All the males were required to go up to Jerusalem three times a year to celebrate their national feasts, leaving their property and families in a defenceless state, surrounded on every side by enemies—God having promised that on such occasions he would restrain their enemies from invading them. Now, no lawgiver without divine sanction would have ventured such an enactment. This is positive proof that Moses received authority from God to incorporate this law into his code.

THE MORAL LAW.

There is found in this wonderful code what is denominated the moral law—the most marvellous compend of duty to be found in the whole range of literature or law. It is a code absolutely perfect. There is nothing like it. Whence did Moses get such a law, but from God? It could not have come from any other source. It sweeps the whole field of man's relations to God and to his fellow-man. Nothing is left out. Not all the wisdom of the world has ever been able to suggest any amendment. It stands all alone in its stately grandeur, unapproached and unapproachable. It is alike the wonder and astonishment of jurists, statesmen, philosophers and theologians. Here we have a standard—a perfect rule by which to measure our heart and conduct; a rule so strict and rigid that it suffers no deviation whatever from its requirements of absolute love to God and man, for this is its summary. The law is strictly and rigidly just, for men ought to love God with the supreme affections of their hearts, and they ought to love their fellow-men. Reason and conscience alike approve this. Now, the law being just, being strict and extending its claims over all rational intelligences, and being the very foundation of God's moral and spiritual government over the universe, must have a penalty corresponding to its purity and importance. This is death—death in its deepest sense and widest sweep. Death temporal, death spiritual and death eternal are all involved in it. Nothing less could have been an adequate expression on the part of an infinitely holy God for the transgression of an infinitely holy law. This law is so transcendent—taking cognizance of the thoughts, feelings and affections of the heart as well as the outward acts of life—no man has ever kept or can keep it. Now, either man made this law or God made it. But it is positively certain man would not make a law he could not keep and then annex the penalty of death for not keeping it, therefore God must have made it. If God made it, then it is divine, and the book that contains it is from heaven.

PROPHECY.

Here I shall be very brief, as I do not wish to present anything the truth of which you can not verify.

Deut. 28:52, 53—You will read: Thou shalt be removed into all the kingdoms of the earth, and thou shalt become an astonishment, a proverb and a byword among all nations whither the Lord shall lead thee. Here is the prediction uttered and recorded thousands of years ago. Look around you on every side and see its exact fulfillment. Indeed, do you not yourself furnish evidence of its accomplishment. Have you not often yourself read the expression, "As rich as a Jew," "As close as a Jew," thus using the term "Jew" as a byword.

Turn and read the entire chapter referred to above and see how exactly it has been fulfilled in the history of this wonderful people.

AUTHORITY OF THE BIBLE. 31

Lev. 26:44. Notwithstanding all their persecutions and sufferings they were not to be utterly destroyed. This accounts for their continuance through all the ages. In fact, it is utterly impossible for the *combined powers of the world to destroy them*. They are the "bush on fire," but never consumed. They live, and will continue to live, witnessing to all the nations of the earth the unity of the divine nature, the moral grandeur of their religion, and the superintendence of God over the affairs of earth. God has sifted them, but *you* had better let the Jew alone.

A few reflections respecting this people may not be out of place.

There is nothing in the history of the world so striking, so impressive, so astonishing as the preservation of this strange race. It is without any parallel in the annals of earth. It can not be accounted for upon any known principles governing human actions. We must accept the direct interposition of God in their perpetuation as the only solution of the problem. And in doing this we must accept the divine origin of the book that records these facts. Always, comparatively speaking, a small and weak nation, occupying a very limited territory, with manners, customs and institutions peculiar to themselves, and a religion different from all others. Yet they have outlived all the mighty monarchies and empires of antiquity, and seem to be well nigh endowed with *indestructibility*. They have been emphatically a wandering people. They have wandered all over the world. Their progenitors, Abraham, Isaac and Jacob, were wanderers. They wandered down into Egypt. There they became slaves—emancipated, they took up their line of march and followed the cloudy pillar by day and the pillar of fire by night through the deserts of Arabia to the promised land. They have seen the great monarchy of Egypt and the empires of Assyria, Babylon and Persia rise, flourish and pass away. They were an old nation when Alexander carried his conquering banners to India; when Romulus founded Rome; lived through all the career of this wonderful government, and saw it go down in darkness and blood. They lived through all the stirring and startling events of the middle ages; saw the Crusaders pour their millions of mailed warriors upon the plains of Asia to wrest from the Moslem the sepulcher of the Savior. O Jew, thou hast been everywhere. Everywhere peeled, and scathed, and scattered. Everywhere scorned, persecuted and oppressed! When the Man of Sorrow stood before the Roman governor and the latter inquired, "Whom will ye that I release unto you, Barabbas or Jesus, which is called Christ?" thou didst say, "Barabbas." Pilate saith unto them, "What, then, shall I do with him whom ye call the

King of the Jews?" Thou didst cry, "Crucify him! Crucify him!" And when the governor took water and washed his hands, saying, "I am innocent of the blood of this just person, see ye to it;" thou didst say, "Let his blood be upon us and our children." O what a malediction! What an accomplishment! Thou didst mock the dying agonies of the Son of God! Thou hast since walked the earth in sadness and sorrow. Thou hast seen thy glorious temple with its lofty battlements, gleaming and glittering with gold and jewels, laid low in the dust. And Jerusalem! What memories are awakened by this hallowed name! Jerusalem, the city of prophets! apostles, martyrs—razed to the ground, swept by the besom of destruction. O Jew, awful has been thy sins! *Terrible has been thy punishment!* Thy blood has been shed upon a thousand hills! watered a thousand plains! dyed a thousand rivers! Thy children sold into slavery or given to strangers, thy property confiscated! wife torn from thy embrace! thyself shut up in gloomy dungeons or dying in torture! Like Noah's dove, thou findest no rest for the sole of thy foot, and wilt not until thou repent and accept the "Crucified." Then peace and prosperity will return unto thee, and thou shalt love and serve God on earth, and, dying, thou shalt have a home in heaven with Abraham, Isaac and Jacob.

I think no candid mind can examine the facts

and arguments presented and deny that the religion of the Jews is divine, and that they have been under the special care and protection of the Almighty.

I have not presented a tithe of the evidence at her hands. I have been compelled to be as brief as possible. But if one will not be convinced by what has been advanced, neither would he be satisfied though "one should rise from the dead." If he rejects all this testimony, he has great reason to fear that he is given over to hardness of heart and reprobacy of mind, and left to believe a lie that he may be damned. It is a *fearful* thing to close the eyes, stop the ears and *harden* the heart against the truth. My dear sir, it is a fearfully dangerous position to occupy. If you don't retreat from it and repent, God will call away his Spirit, leave you to die in your folly and be damned in hell forever.

There is one more thought I will suggest before closing this chapter. And that is, that the Jews, though without a land and without a government, few, feeble and scattered, yet are they the most powerful people in the world, in that they hold the purse strings of all the civilized nations of earth. They can say to them, "Thus far and no farther," and the mightiest governments must respect their decree. The weakest, and yet the strongest. Strange anomaly!

CHAPTER IV.

DIVINITY OF CHRIST.

NOW, some nineteen hundred years ago there appeared in the land of Judea a most extraordinary person claiming to be the Son of God. He said that he was sent into the world to redeem it from the curse of sin and to restore it to the divine favor. And it is very remarkable that in the ancient records of the people of that country there are the clearest intimations that in the future ages such a character should make his appearance, and so strong a hold had this idea gained in the minds of the people that there was a general expectation that the time had arrived for the realization of this hope. His parentage was very humble—being born of a mother who, though of an illustrious family, had fallen into poverty and obscurity. Growing up into manhood, he became the most wonderful teacher in the world. Every thing recorded of him is in harmony with his claim of being divine. There was no sin in his life; no impurity in his soul; no selfish ambition; no aspirations after the wealth, honors and applause of the world. He rebuked sin everywhere. He was humble, tender and compassionate; and, at the same time, lofty and dignified. In a word, his life furnished a perfect pattern of holiness and purity. His wisdom surpassed that of all other men. He was never deceived by flattery, cajoled by caresses, or awed by power. Of all the teeming millions of earth, he stood out all alone in the dignity of his person, the purity of his life, the benevolence of his character, the marvels of his wisdom, and the grandeur of his works. Such is a faint outline of the character of Jesus Christ, who claimed to be the Son of God.

Now, if this claim can be substantiated, if he was really divine, God over all blessed for evermore, then it follows with irresistible certainty that the book that contains his life and character is likewise divine, for it has his unqualified endorsement.

Let us briefly survey the evidences.

We go back to the oldest records of time—the Jewish sacred books. We there learn that upon the fall of man a promise was made that "the seed of the woman should bruise the serpent's head." Here is the first intimation of this coming personage.

Turning over a little further, we see the patriarch, Jacob, in blessing his children, declares that "the scepter shall not depart from Judah, nor a lawgiver from between his feet, till Shiloh shall come, and to him shall the gathering of the people be." Here is a further development of the same idea. Reading on, we come to another wonderful prediction by Moses, the great Jewish leader. In giving instruction to his people, he says, "The Lord your God shall raise up unto you a prophet like unto me, him shall ye hear in all things, and it shall come to pass that whosoever will not hear that prophet shall be cut off from among the people." These and many similar predictions are sufficient to show the grounds of the Jewish faith in the coming Messiah. The place of his birth was foretold—it was to be in Bethlehem of Judea; likewise the time of his birth was predicted. In fact, all his leading characteristics were described. All these found an exact fulfillment in the life and work of Christ.

There were many personal types of Christ, such as Abraham, Isaac, Joseph, David, Solomon, Joshua, all possessing some leading feature pointing to Christ. When Christ came, all these particulars found their fulfillment and illustration in him.

What an array of evidence, what overwhelming testimony to the fact that Christ was the Holy One of God.

Besides the many personal types alluded to above, there were many others that were exceedingly striking and impressive. Of which none was more so than the Passover lamb. In this we have an emblem of Christ crucified. The lamb was slain and dressed. It was then pierced lengthwise with a stake, then transfixed through the shoulders with another stake, thus forming a perfect cross. It was then roasted before the fire, expressive of the sufferings of Christ. Not a bone of it was to be broken, corresponding to the fact that not a bone of Christ was broken. It was then eaten, giving strength and vigor to the participants, just as partaking of Christ by faith gives spiritual life and vigor to those exercising that faith.

The brazen serpent was a type of Christ in his saving power. When the Israelites were bitten by the fiery serpents, all they had to do to be healed was to *look* at the brazen serpent; thus showing that the sinner had only to look to Christ for salvation.

The manna showered upon the Israelites in the wilderness was typical of the saving grace of our Lord Jesus Christ who is said to be the bread of life.

The smitten rock typified Christ, "who was wounded for our transgressions and bruised for our iniquities." As the rock when smitten poured out its refreshing waters to revive the thirsty Israelites, so Christ when smitten poured out his life-giving blood for the salvation of sinners. But why enumerate particulars, there are hundreds of them. To mention them all would be to write volumes. In fact, the whole Jewish economy was in a large measure symbolical and illustrative of the work of Christ—his birth, his life, his character, his death, burial, resurrection, ascension, and glorification. The Old Testament is just as full of Christ as the New. The only difference is that in the Old it is veiled in symbol. Now how is it possible that these well nigh innumerable particulars should all find their exact correspondence and fulfillment in Christ, unless he *is divine, unless he is the Son of God?*

I adduce another fact proving his divinity. This fact is different from all other facts in the history of the world. It is the only fact of the kind that ever occurred or ever will occur on earth. And that fact is *Christ voluntarily died for his enemies.* Said he in his teachings, "No GREATER love hath any man than this, that a man lay down his life for his *friends.* This is the utmost reach of human love. But very few instances of this kind have ever occurred. But Christ laid down his life for his *enemies.* This is the only case on record.

Of all the millions of earth no human being has ever been known to voluntarily lay down his life for his enemies. If no mere man has ever been found to do this thing, then Christ was no *mere* man, but was God over all. This argument is absolutely invincible. It admits of no answer or evasion.

THE PARABLES OF CHRIST PROVE HIS DIVINITY.

We find in these pleasing and instructive narratives the very concentration of wisdom and doctrine. They have no parallel in the literature of the world. There is nothing that even approximates them. I challenge all the schools of Europe, America and the world to write just one such parable as the prodigal son. I will stake the whole question upon their inability to do it. What, with two thousand years of learning and study, with all the examples before them, can't write one such parable! No; can't write one such parable. What does this show? Why it shows that it is not within the compass of the human intellect unaided by divine revelation to do this thing. You can not account for this supernal wisdom of Christ upon any other ground than that he was divine, the Messiah—the Son of God.

THE SINLESSNESS OF CHRIST PROVES HIS DIVINITY.

If there is any one fact that towers immeasurably above all other facts respecting the human race it is the fact that man is a sinner. This all systems of religion and philosophy admit. Every government on earth is based upon this assumption. The universal consciousness of the race convicts man as a wrong-doer.

Now how did it happen that amidst sweeping, devouring, corroding corruption; corruption of high life and low life; corruption of men, women and children; corruption through all the ages; corruption everywhere; corruption deep, dark and damning; a seething caldron of moral putridity. I ask how did it happen that we find only *one* wearing the human garb, clothed in mortal flesh, that escaped the contamination and pollution everywhere prevalent? *The infidel must answer this question.* Let there be no shirking or evasion. We will accept none. He must answer this question or confess his utter inability to do it. If he can't answer it, his whole system breaks down and becomes a hopeless wreck. He can never answer it; *never, while the sun and moon endure; never, while the stars shine; never, while the wind blows and the tides flow.*

But Christianity can answer, the Bible can answer it. It says Jesus Christ was the Son of God, the brightness of the Father's glory and the express image of his person. He took upon himself our nature, was tempted like as we are, yet *without sin.* This is the answer, the only one that can or ever will be given.

THE MIRACLES OF CHRIST PROVE HIS DIVINITY.

The most stupendous miracles are ascribed to Christ. With a touch, or a word, he cured all manner of diseases, restored sight to the blind, hearing to the deaf, and life to the dead. He stilled the raging billows, hushed the howling tempest, and fed thousands with a few loaves and fishes. Now, if he really wrought these deeds, no one will question that he was divine, was the Son of God. The miracles performed were so numerous, so public, so palpable, that there could be no deception about them. They were either solemn verities or unmitigated shams. That they could not have been the latter is evident from their nature and all the attendant circumstances. They were performed in open day—in the presence of keen, shrewd and captious enemies, who were bitter and unrelenting foes of Christ. If they had been impositions, surely those opponents would have found it out and exposed it. In fact, the *very character of those miracles* themselves render such a supposition out of the question. Surely the hungry multitudes knew whether or not they partook of the loaves and fishes and were satisfied. Surely the blind knew when the light of day visited their darkened orbs. Surely the deaf knew when the sweet melody of sounds and the voice of love and friendship saluted their

AUTHORITY OF THE BIBLE.

ears. That they were actually wrought, we have the testimony of both friends and foes who were present and were eyewitnesses. The Pharisees themselves admitted their reality. And in the whole history of those times there is no counter testimony. The evidence, then, is most conclusive that Christ wrought those miracles attributed to him; and if he did he was divine, he was the Son of God.

THE TESTIMONY OF ANGELS.

Luke 2:9, 10, 11. And, lo, the angel of the Lord came upon them (the shepherds), and the glory of the Lord shone round about them; and they were sore afraid. And the angel said unto them, Fear not: for, behold, I bring you good tidings of great joy, which shall be to all people. For unto you is born this day in the city of David a Savior, which is Christ the Lord.

THE TESTIMONY OF THE FATHER.

Mark 1:10. And straightway coming up out of the water, he saw the heavens opened, and there came a voice, saying, Thou art my beloved Son, in whom I am well pleased.

THE TESTIMONY OF THE HOLY SPIRIT.

Luke 3:22. And the Holy Spirit descended in a bodily shape like a dove upon him.

TESTIMONY OF PILATE'S WIFE.

When Jesus was apprehended and on trial, the wife of Pilate, with that strange intuition so characteristic of women, sent word to him "to have nothing to do with that just person." But just he could not have been unless he was what he claimed to be, the Son of God.

Pilate himself, after an examination, testified, "I find no fault in him."

THE TESTIMONY OF THE CENTURION.

When the Roman officer who superintended the crucifixion of Christ saw the remarkable phenomena attending his death—the preturnatural darkness and earthquake—he exclaimed, "Truly this was the Son of God." Surely the opinion of this witness is entitled to a great deal of weight, as he must have known a great deal about Christ's character and claims.

THE TESTIMONY OF JUDAS.

Judas was one of the twelve apostles. He was intimately associated with Christ for years. He knew him as well as one can know another. Had there been anything in the life and character of the latter inimical to his claims of being the Son of God, he would assuredly have pleaded it in justification of his betrayal. Suffer a little digression here. It has been thought strange by some that Christ should have chosen so bad a man as Judas as one of his apostles. Let me suggest he was chosen because he was a *suitable person to act the traitor.* He was *willing* to do it. *He was the very man for the occasion.* Here we see God's sovereignty in using a bad man to accomplish his own divine purposes. Judas was *guilty* because he acted voluntarily and without constraint. He did the deed of his own free will and choice. After seeing the ruin he had wrought, he was seized with undying remorse. With hell-dogs barking at his heels and the vulture of despair dipping his bloody beak into his heart; no longer able to endure life, he leaps into hell, crying, "I have sinned in that I have betrayed innocent 'blood.'" But innocent blood it could not have been unless Christ was what he declared himself to be, the Son of God.

THE TESTIMONY OF DEMONS.

Mark 3:11. And unclean spirits, when they saw him, fell down before him, and cried, saying, "Thou art the Son of God."

THE TESTIMONY OF CHRIST HIMSELF.

He himself bore witness constantly to the fact that he was the Son of God.

THE TESTIMONY OF NATURE AT HIS CRUCIFIXION PROVES HIS DIVINITY.

The death of Christ was the most remarkable event in the history of the world. It was the fulfillment of all the prophecies, the consummation of all the types of the Mosaic dispensation. It was the end of the Old and the beginning of a New era. It was indispensable to the vindication of God's law, the manifestation of his justice, the display of his wisdom, the exhibition of his mercy, and the salvation of sinners. It contains more elements of pathos and of moral grandeur and power than any other event that ever took place. The natural tendency of harshness and the infliction of suffering is to harden the heart and render obdurate the will. On the contrary, the natural tendency of gentle, suffering love is to change the affections, subdue the will, and bring about reconciliation. Consequently we see that the Christian scheme is naturally adapted to bless and save the race. The exhibition of God's love in the gift and death of his Son presents all the motives that can be brought to bear to secure the affections and obedience of man to God and his government.

There hangs upon the cross the bleeding victim. See! how his head reels! How his temples throb! How his veins swell! Hark! There comes a cry from the sufferer: "Father, forgive them; for they know not what they do." But what means this gathering gloom? What mean these darkened heavens and trembling earth? What mean these rending rocks, and opening graves, and rising dead? Jesus suffers! One long hour is ended and another begins. How his blood pours in fiery currents through his tortured veins. But, hush! There is another cry from the dying victim: "My God, my God, why hast thou forsaken me?" It was a cry of anguish—a cry of loneliness and desolation. Another hour closes—the last begins. But mark the sufferer is sinking—lower, lower, lower. Death is drawing its prophetic film over his languid eyes—pulse intermitting—fluttering—muscles relaxing. But list! one more cry: "Father, into thy hands I commend my spirit;" and he is beyond the pain and anguish of the cross, and the envy and malice of the howling mob. What a scene! What an event! Was nature ever before thrown into such tumult at the death of any other person? Never, never. Heroes have fallen in battle for their country; statesmen have perished at their posts in vindicating the rights of their nation; millions of martyrs have gone shouting home to glory from the dungeon, the scaffold, and the stake, but never in one instance has the placidity of nature been disturbed. But when Christ died all nature was convulsed. The sun refused to shine when the greater light of earth was darkening in death; the earth shook; rocks rent; the graves were opened and the dead arose. What a testimony is here presented in favor of the divinity of Christ?

CHRIST'S PROPHECIES STAMP HIM AS DIVINE.

The limits allowed us compel us to be very brief on this line of our inquiry.

I call your attention to that remarkable prophecy of the Savior respecting the destruction of Jerusalem and the overthrow of the Jewish state, together with the accompanying signs and prodigies which attended them. These predictions are very explicit, and are found recorded in the 24th chapter of Matt., 13th chapter of Mark, and the 17th and 21st chapter of Luke.

Luke gives it thus: "And they shall fall by the edge of the sword, and shall be led away captive into all nations: and Jerusalem shall be trodden down of the Gentiles, until the times of the Gentiles be fulfilled. And there shall be signs in the sun, and in the moon and in the stars; and upon the earth distress of nations with perplexity; the sea and the waves roaring; men's hearts failing them for fear, and for looking after those things which are coming on the earth."

The signs and precursors of these events were to be false Christs; seditions and wars; famines and pestilences, earthquakes and extraordinary

AUTHORITY OF THE BIBLE.

appearances in the heavens, etc.,—the utter destruction of the temple, so that not one stone should be left on another.

So much now for the prophecy. Now for the fulfillment. Josephus, the Jewish historian, who was a witness of what he records, and was present and participated in the startling events of the siege and fall of Jerusalem, tells us that imposters and magicians drew multitudes into the wilderness, promising to show them signs and wonders.

Theudas was another who pretended to be a prophet, and gave out that he would divide the waters of the Jordan. In fact, the whole land was overrun by imposters and false Christs. Wars and seditions convulsed the land. Both Josephus and Philo give an account of these disturbances in which multitudes of people perished. Gaunt famine stalked at midnight; pestilence wasted at noonday; and earthquakes shook the land. These facts are mentioned by Suetonius, by Josephus, by Tacitus and Seneca. Josephus and Tacitus both tell us that prodigies were frequent. The former declares that a star hung over the city like a sword for a whole year; that at the ninth hour of the night a bright light shone around the altar and the temple, so that for the space of half an hour it appeared to be bright day; that the eastern gate of the temple, which required twenty men to shut, and which was fastened by strong bars and bolts, opened of its own accord; that before sunset there was seen in the clouds the appearance of chariots and armies fighting; that at the feast of Pentecost, while the priests were going into the inner temple, a voice was heard as of a multitude saying, "Let us depart hence."

And what affected the people more than anything else was, that four years after the war began, a countryman came to Jerusalem, at the feast of Tabernacles, and run up and down crying day and night, "A voice from the east, a voice from the west, a voice from the four winds, a voice against Jerusalem and the temple. Wo! wo to Jerusalem!" It was in vain that by stripes and torture the magistrates attempted to restrain him. He continued crying for seven years and five months, and yet never grew hoarse nor appeared to be weary, until during the siege, while he was crying on the wall a stone struck him and he was instantly killed. Tacitus, the Roman historian, joins his testimony to that of Josephus. Jerusalem finally fell, being hemmed in on all sides by the besieging army, while famine, pestilence and tumult raged within. Finally the temple was burned, and the very ground on which it stood was plowed up; and the remnant of the people carried away captives into all nations, where they continue as strangers and pilgrims to this day. Who can read this wonderful prophecy of the Savior and its exact fulfillment and doubt his divinity?

THE RESURRECTION OF CHRIST PROVES HIS DIVINITY.

There is no question as to the death and burial of Christ. But did he rise from the dead? This is the keystone to the arch. If the proof fails here the whole fabric tumbles into ruins. If he did rise, then he was the Son of God, and his claims of being divine is placed upon an immovable foundation; and Christianity is from heaven and the Bible is divinely inspired. The most confirmed skeptic will admit that if he rose from the dead his claims have the highest attestation possible. What evidence, then, have we of this fact? I answer, the testimony of those who were intimately acquainted with him—who had spent years in his companionship, journeyed with him, ate with him and received instruction from his lips. These men aver that *after his death and burial* they saw him, handled him, conversed with him, received instruction from him for forty days and then saw him ascend to heaven in their presence. Were these competent witnesses? None could possibly be more so. These were plain, unsophisticated, matter-of-fact men, whose hardy outdoor life had fully developed their senses of hearing and seeing. They testified only to what they saw, and heard, and felt, and *absolutely knew.* There is no room to suppose that they were deceived. They could not have been deceived. If they were, then the senses furnish no criterion for the truth of anything. If they were deceived, then you have to account for the fact that practical, sensible men for the space of forty days thought they saw what they never saw, thought they heard what they never heard, and witnessed what never occurred. You must believe this or accept their testimony to the fact of Christ's resurrection. In this discussion there is only one thing for the opposition to do, either to accept the resurrection of Christ as a fact, or to ignore all reason and all laws governing the human mind and human conduct.

Were these witnesses *sincere?* There is no ground to mistrust their sincerity. They furnish the very highest proof possible to be given of their sincerity. In the face of danger, obloquy, persecution, hatred and universal opposition, they took their lives in their hands and went forth proclaiming everywhere the resurrection of Christ, and at last laid down *their lives* in attestation of this fact. If anything can be proved by human testimony, then is it proved that Jesus rose from the dead. And if he rose from the dead, he has the attestation of heaven itself that he was the Son of God.

Another proof that Christ rose from the dead

AUTHORITY OF THE BIBLE.

is the change of the seventh day, the Jewish Sabbath, to the first day of the week as a day of rest. This was done to commemorate the fact that Jesus rose from the dead on this day. To perpetuate this fact, the disciples from the very beginning observed the *first day* of the week. Hence this observance has come down to us through all intervening ages and stands as a perpetual proof to all people of the resurrection of Jesus.

In the act of baptism we have symbolized the great facts of the death, burial and *resurrection* of Christ.

We have, then, not only the testimony of personal eyewitnesses to this fact, but in addition thereto two monumental institutions, Sunday and Baptism, testifying to the same fact. Against this tremendous array of proof there is absolutely no counter testimony. The evidence adduced establishes beyond controversy the fact that Jesus rose from the dead, and hence he is the Son of God, and by consequence the Bible is divine, because it is full of Christ from Genesis to Revelation.

CHAPTER V.

THE DOCTRINES OF THE BIBLE ARE INCORPORATED INTO AND PERMEATE THE WHOLE FABRIC OF HUMAN AFFAIRS.

I WISH now, by another and independent line of argument, to show that the doctrines of the Bible are incorporated into and permeate the whole fabric of human affairs, and that they are received and acted upon in all temporal matters by the whole human race. In a word, that every man, woman and child through all the ages is fully committed to these doctrines and can not object to one of them without at the same time condemning himself. This is a very strange and wonderful arrangement, and seems hitherto to have escaped observation. To give you, in a sentence, the trend of the argument I am going to make, I will state that as the great laws of Nature, such as electricity, magnetism, heat, gravity, etc., pervade all material bodies; so the principles of the Bible run through all human affairs, and are interwoven into the very fabric and constitution of things. God has not left himself without witness as to the truth of his Word, but has so arranged things as to make his foes as well as his friends to testify to its truth.

REPENTANCE.

Let us begin with the doctrine of repentance and see how far all men are committed to it. The Scriptures teach that in order to pardon, the sinner must repent—that is, change his mind and change his conduct—must turn about from a course of sin to a course of uprightness. Now, do not all men require this of those who have offended them? This is always and everywhere a condition of reconciliation between parties at variance. So long as the offending party continues his offenses, reconciliation is out of the question. But the moment he changes his course, peace between the two becomes practicable. Other elements of repentance are that the offender confess his fault, express sorrow for it, and ask forgiveness. No man requires more than this in order to the restoration of friendship. The duelist upon the deadly field only asks for an apology—a confession from his antagonist. This done, peace is restored. Now, with what consistency can any man object to the Scriptural doctrine of repentance, seeing God in this requires of every wrongdoer just what every man requires of those that have trespassed against him. The principles embraced in the doctrine of repentance are every man's principles, and are universally recognized. *These principles are founded in the nature of things and ac-*

cord with man's mental and moral constitution, and it is impossible for alienated friendship to be restored in any other way.

FAITH.

The Bible dwells with much emphasis upon faith. It ascribes a great deal of power and efficacy to it. It represents it as indispensable to our acceptance with God. It is the channel through which comes spiritual light and life. It is not an arbitrary principle introduced into the divine scheme without reason, but is based upon the profoundest philosophy. As a regulator of human conduct it is the most powerful force that can be brought to bear. Men act, when they act consistently, in accordance with what they believe. Hence it controls, in a large measure, the actions of men. It likewise governs the conscience, the conscience sometimes approving in one what it condemns in another, because of difference in their beliefs. It likewise governs the affections. If you *believe* an object to be good, your affections are naturally drawn out towards it. If you believe it to be bad, your aversion towards it is excited. Another fact, we become more assimilated in character to those objects in which we have the most faith. Hence it would be impossible to be saved unless we have a holy object (God) set before us as the object of faith to control our actions, call forth our affections, and purify our conscience. Such is the transcendent importance of faith as set forth in the Bible. The belief of *truth* is always promotive of man's highest interest and happiness, whereas the belief of falsehood is always misleading and ruinous. Now, if we will turn our eyes to human affairs, we will find its power and influence just as great. Without it no government can exist, no society, no association of any kind, no banks, no business, no money, no family, no social relations. Strike down the cohesive power of faith and you toll the death knell of the race in regard to all temporal affairs. Universal disaster and ruin would ensue just as the Bible says follows the absence of faith in reference to spiritual affairs. Thus we see the Bible in no respect exaggerates its importance—just as necessary in the affairs of this life as in that which is to come. It is a principle universally accepted and acted upon by the whole human race. It is one of the moral forces of the universe, and holds that relation to spiritual things that gravity does to material things. It is incorporated into the very constitution of nature, and the infidel is as much committed to it as the Christian.

PRAYER.

The Bible teaches the doctrine and duty of prayer. All the great characters of the Bible were noted for their prayerfulness. Christ both taught and exemplified it—sometimes spending the whole night in supplicating the divine throne. Now there is a deep philosophy in prayer. It is the highest form of worship. It is an acknowledgment of God's existence and sovereignty, and our weakness and dependence. It involves a confession of our sinfulness, our sorrow for it, and our desire for deliverance from it. Where these feelings are sincere and earnest, they necessarily lift the suppliant up into communion with God and conformity to his will. No one can possibly grow in the divine life without prayer. It is one of the appointed means for spiritual growth. It is adapted to this end, because it brings us in contact with the divine Being and holds us there till we catch something of his heavenly effulgence and glory. We must be in *touch* with objects before they can affect us or we influence them. Hence people living in close and intimate relations for years come to resemble each other and to partake very much of each others characteristics.

Prayer then is not only Scriptural, but is founded in the nature of things.

Now let us see how far this doctrine is interwoven in the affairs of life. Every one that ever petitioned a court or a legislative body for the granting of a favor, the removal of a grievance, or the pardon of a criminal, did in that act, commit himself to the Bible doctrine of prayer. Hence it is that no one can call in question the teaching of the Scriptures on this point, without at the same time condemning himself.

ETERNAL PUNISHMENT.

There is no doctrine of the Scriptures that has met with fiercer denunciation and more bitter opposition than that stated above. But denunciation and opposition prove nothing. Is the Scriptural teaching on this question true? If it is I want to know it so that I may shun so sad a catastrophe. The Christian church through all the ages has understood that the fate of the finally impenitent was one of unmitigated horror, one of eternal doom, one of utter and hopeless ruin. She has never shirked from this doctrine nor failed on all suitable occasions to affirm it.

Now if this be the correct interpretation of the Scriptures we may expect to find the same principle imbedded in the affairs around us. For God has arranged the things of earth so as to cause all men to accept and act out the very principles he has embodied in his word. The Bible recognizes a radical and essential difference between truth and error, an antagonism that is irreconcilable. This fact is confirmed by the experience of the whole race. This being admitted, it follows that truth and error being so opposite in their nature, can not lead to the same result. The outcome must be different. If virtue leads to heaven and happiness, vice must lead to hell and misery. If the happiness of one is eternal, the misery of the other must be likewise. This all accords with the analogies of nature. In human affairs there are often points reached from which there is no return; results achieved for which there is no remedy. A ball crashing through the brain ends life; a man standing on a precipice and taking one more step is hurled into the abyss and lost. In these and a thousand similar instances the ruin is irretrievable; it is utter and hopeless. So in the downward course of the sinner, he finally reaches a point where the mercy of God can not reach him and he is eternally lost. He has passed out of the present condition of things into a new order where no provision is made for restoration and where no mercy can be exercised. You ask, why so direful a result? I answer why so direful a result oftentimes from the incidents of this life? I answer again, it is inevitable. It could not be otherwise. It finds its basis in the character of God who is infinitely opposed to sin, and who did all that could be done in a moral government to prevent its entrance, and after its entrance has done all that could be done to mitigate its effects and to extirpate it from the world. He inquires, "What could I have done more to my vineyard that I have not done?" He has reasoned, warned, expostulated, entreated. Sent his Son to die upon the cross; given his Word to enlighten, his Spirit to convince, and sent his ministers to proclaim the terms of peace and pardon, and to offer a blissful immortality beyond the grave upon the simple terms of accepting the remedy he himself has provided and offered. To all his proffered mercies men turn away their ears and scoff and scorn. God's offers are derided, despised and rejected, his mercy scouted, his majesty insulted, his laws trampled under foot, and his government dishonored. What else could he do after exhausting all the resources of parental love, but let the thunderbolt fall?

This state of things finds its parallel in the history of thousands of families in this world. the gray-haired father sees his beloved children enter upon a course of vice and folly which he knows will result in their ruin. He admonishes, warns, prays and entreats; but all in vain. They give no heed, lift no cry to God for help, but plunge along in their wild and wicked career until death closes the scene and hell swallows them up. Whose fault? Evidently their own. So with the finally impenitent sinner. You thus see the very same principles hold their sway in this world as are set forth in the Bible. Whoever established the one established the other.

Let us elaborate this matter a little further and show that every human being since the fall of Adam is fully committed by his own personal acts to this principle of "everlasting banishment from the presence of the Lord and the glory of his power." Every government has found it necessary to cut off incorrigible offenders from citizenship, either by taking their lives or shutting them up in prison as long as they live—that is forever, so far as this world is concerned. Now, no one objects to this principle in human governments. Why should they object to it in the divine government? If it is right and necessary in the one, it is equally so in the other. If you admit it in one, you must allow it in the other. There is no escape from this conclusion. It is the experience of the world that this is necessary in civil government, and it has received the sanction and endorsement of all ages. If so, it is equally necessary in God's government. The world is not only committed in the *mass* to this doctrine, but each *individual* is *personally* committed to it. Did you ever crush a fly, a flea, or other insect? If you did, you cut it off *for ever* from all *life, liberty* and *enjoyment.* Here *you* claim and exercise the very same right you deny to the Almighty Ruler of the universe. I ask the infidel what he will do with the cold-hearted, red-handed murderer. I will rest the whole

AUTHORITY OF THE BIBLE.

issue upon his answer. He can not possibly answer it without ruining his system. If he says he would execute him, well, that is cutting him off *for ever* from all life and liberty. If he says he would shut him up in prison for life, that is just what the Bible says. If he answers he would do nothing, then that is the end of law and government and the introduction of universal anarchy. Thus you see that all governments, human and divine, have found this principle a necessary element in their structure. Let there, then, be no objection to the doctrine of eternal punishment as set forth in the Bible. The moment one objects to it, he condemns himself.

It is sometimes urged that there is no proportion between the time of committing the deed and the penalty. I answer, neither is there in human governments. Time is not an element in assessing the punishment. A man may in *one moment* commit an act that will forfeit his life, or send him to the penitentiary as long as he lives.

THE ATONEMENT.

There is something very wonderful about blood. I don't know what it is; but there is something very wonderful about blood. See how the noble horse starts and trembles when he catches the scent of it. See how the beasts of the menagerie are aroused and pace their cages when its odor is wafted to their nostrils! See how the cattle paw the ground and utter mournful lamentations and loud bellowings when they smell it. *There is something very wonderful about blood.* I do not know what it is. Look at the man that has shed it wrongfully. The stain is upon his hand, the blight is upon his heart! To get rid of it, he climbs the mountain heights, plunges into the valleys low, crosses the wide, wide ocean; but the stain is upon his hand, the blight is upon his heart. The specter of his murdered victim walks by his side, comes in the midnight hour and peers reproachfully into his eyes, lays his cold and skeleton fingers upon his brow until the soul of the man is wracked with horror and he quivers like an aspen. Yes; there is something very wonderful about blood. Now, the Scriptures tell us, "without the shedding of blood there is no remission." They cleave to the soul through everlasting ages, no forgiveness, no peace with God, no hope of heaven. We are further told that "the blood of Jesus cleanses from all sin." Through the application of it by the Spirit the conscience is purified and spiritual and divine life is given.

Now let us see if we can not find in the things around us an exact counterpart of this--a counterpart so exact, a practice so general as to commit the whole race to this principle.

AUTHORITY OF THE BIBLE.

The noble ox and the innocent lamb must give up their lives, must die, must shed their blood that we may live temporarily and physically. So Christ gave up his life, shed his blood, that we may live spiritually and eternally. The one dies for our physical well-being, the other dies for our spiritual well-being. Christ died a violent death, poured out his blood. So animals must die a violent death—shed their blood—otherwise their flesh is not suitable for human food. The antithesis is direct—the parallelism is perfect. You accept the one and act upon it, therefore you are compelled to accept the other. Every thing that sustains our bodies implies the death of that thing. With what propriety, then, can any one slaughter an animal and *live* upon its flesh and at the same time deny that there is any efficacy in the death of Christ?

Thus we see that the doctrines of the Bible are interwoven into the whole structure of things around us, and that men everywhere unconsciously receive and act upon them while they reject the very same principles in the Bible. For this gross inconsistency they alone are responsible. Well do the Scriptures say, "Every mouth shall be shut, and the whole world become guilty before God."

SUBSTITUTION.

Christ took our place under the law, died in our room and stead; died "the just for the unjust;" was wounded for our transgressions; was bruised for our iniquities. He was *our substitute*. This is the teaching of the Scriptures. This doctrine has been strenuously opposed and bitterly denounced both by heretics and infidels; but it is clearly taught in the divine word and is accepted and practiced by all governments and all individuals. It is a primary principle inwrought into the very structure of the universe. It was from a want of understanding this that the devil committed the sad mistake of introducing death into the world.

In placing Adam and Eve in the garden, God gave them full permission to eat of the fruit of all the trees with one exception, declaring that if they partook of that tree, they should die. The devil seemed to reason thus with himself: "If I can tempt them to eat the forbidden fruit and thus transgress God's law, God must be true to his promise and cut them off and thus his whole plan of creation will be frustrated. Or if he does not cut them off, he stands before the universe dishonored in annexing a penalty to his law he had not the firmness to execute." From his standpoint his reasoning was clear and logical. He saw no escape from the dilemma. But he was caught in his own snare. He was entrapped and ruined by his own scheme. He had left out a very important element in the count, that of substitution. God had embodied this principle in nature. Thus the loss of the eyesight is supplemented in a large measure by increased sensibility in the sense of feeling. Suppression of perspiration is taken up and borne by the lungs or some other organ. In the absence of sunlight, we substitute light from lamps, gas, or electricity. When we have not sufficient heat from the sun to warm us, we kindle fires in its place. And so on throughout the whole constitution of things. Substitution then is a primary element in the universe.

People sometimes seem to think that the fall of man was wholly unlooked for and unprepared for; that it was an exigency in the divine government that perplexed the Creator to meet. Whereas the whole thing was foreseen, provided for, and the world was created so as to harmonize with that condition of things. Hence you see how it was the devil was misled. Instead of thwarting God's purposes he confirmed them. Instead of advancing his own kingdom he ruined it; for the death of Christ overthrows the kingdom of darkness.

Christ, our substitute, took our place and died for us, and thus honored the law. What is done by a substitute or representative being is of the same binding force as when done by the original. And this was no arbitrary arrangement, but was in accordance with the original constitution of things. There was nothing new introduced, nor was there any departure from law and order, but was in strict harmony with both.

I will now briefly show that this principle is accepted and acted upon by the whole race; that it permeates the whole range of human interests, and that no man can deny it any more than he can deny his own existence. It is every man's doctrine confirmed by innumerable acts of his own. All business transactions are but an *exchange of one thing for another, or the substituting of one thing and taking another equivalent to it.* This is precisely what took place in the divine transaction. The sinner was released, let go, and Christ was taken in his stead. In times of war this principle finds an apt illustration: A man is conscripted, all he has to do to keep out of the army is to furnish a *substitute—one to take his place—*who, if he dies in the service or is killed in battle, the principal is regarded as dead, and the law has no further claims upon him. I might show in every man's life almost countless examples in confirmation of what has been stated. If one ever employed a physician, he had to substitute his money for his services. If he ever engaged a lawyer to defend him, he had to give in exchange an equivalent. So of mechanics, artists, laborers.

As originally constituted language was out of harmony with the balance of creation. Unity in language—variety everywhere else. There was but *one* language. Hence with this arrangement there was no room for the principle of exchange or substitution of a word in one language for an equivalent word in another language. To obviate this difficulty, God, at Babel, made other languages, and thus made room for the introduction of substitution. He thus accomplished, by one act, the voluntary dispersion of the people, and at the same time made room for substitution where it was before wanting.

We thus see that God in his wisdom has left all men without any excuse whatever in rejecting the teachings of the Scripture. For the very things they object to they have been practicing all their lives.

God needs no witnesses against any man, for he has so ordered things as to make every one *testify against and condemn himself by his own acts.*

MEDIATION.

But let us advance a little farther in our inquiries and see whether there are not other great Scriptural doctrines which men reject, while at the same time they observe them in the everyday affairs of life.

Christ is represented as our *mediator*—as coming in between an offended God and offending man to make peace—to satisfy the demands of law and thus bring about reconciliation. He came to turn aside from us the consequences of violated moral law and to restore us to spiritual health. We find an exact parallel to this in the physician who comes in to save us from the consequences of violated physiological law and restore us to physical health; likewise the lawyer who mediates to save us from the effects of transgressed civil law and bring about harmonious relations with the government.

Persons at variance are oftentimes reconciled by the intervention of a mutual friend. This principle is extending its influence amongst the nations and is gaining a strong hold upon them. It is being discovered that national disputes should be settled by arbitration, or by reference of the matter to a mediatorial tribunal which will adjust the difference upon the basis of right and justice. Thus as we advance in civilization and spiritual development we begin to see and understand that the principles of the Bible pervade the whole order of things, and that all men are committed to them. No wonder Paul exclaimed, "O the depth of the riches both of the wisdom and knowledge of God."

ADOPTION.

We will now consider for a moment the teaching of the Scriptures in regard to adoption. In our fallen state we are strangers to God and aliens from him. Being regenerated and pardoned we are adopted into the family of God

AUTHORITY OF THE BIBLE.

and become heirs of God and joint heirs with the Lord Jesus Christ, and are entitled to all the privileges and immunities of children. Such is the doctrine of the Scriptures. Now this principle has been accepted and acted upon by all enlightened nations, both of ancient and modern times. The justice and propriety of this have received the sanction and approval of all ages. Now, is this a correct and righteous principle in human governments? If so, is it not likewise in the divine government? If you say yes, then you and the Bible agree. If you say no, then why do you accept it in civil government and ignore it in God's government? If it is right in one, it is likewise right in the other, and consistency requires you to acknowledge it in both.

TRINITY.

It is the distinct and emphatic teaching of the Bible that there is but *one* God. But in this divine unity there are three persons: the Father, the Son, and the Holy Spirit, co-equal and co-eternal. Perhaps no teaching of the Scriptures has been more opposed and denounced by infidels than this. How, say they, can one be three and three be one? Well, I don't know how; nevertheless, I will show you it is a fact. You will find it in your own person. You are but one *person*. Yet, in this one person you will find three distinct persons, closely allied, overlapping, coalescing, inter-penetrating each the other, but yet distinct physical, moral and intellectual. One can not be a man without a physical organization, neither can he be a human being without a *moral* and *intellectual* nature. Yet he is but one man. In your *one* arm you find three divisions—arm, forearm, hand. In fact, man is a trinity all over; head, trunk, limbs; thigh, leg, foot; fingers, first, second, third joints; skin, scarf, true, mucous. So of the trees of the forest—root, body, branches; bark, wood, sap; leaves, flowers, fruits. You thus see that God has not only written this great truth in the Bible, but he has written it in the human constitution and the animal and vegetable kingdoms. Although a little out of place, I will call your attention to another remarkable fact. And that is, man with his arms extended is a *perfect cross*, and that the human face presents a very fair outline of the same figure; the forehead standing for the upper part of the beam, the eyebrows representing the transverse bar, and the nose the lower part. Did all these wonderful coincidences happen by chance? Impossible! God incorporated them into the very nature of things that they might be confirmatory and illustrative of his Word. Hence the conclusion is inevitable and irresistible that whoever made man and the material world made the Bible.

PERSEVERANCE.

Well, you say, how will you get an argument out of this to prove the divine origin and authority of the Bible? Wait and see, and I will get not only an argument, but a *demonstration* of the divine authorship of the Bible.

It has been charged that the Scriptures were inconsistent and contradictory in their teaching upon the subject of man's continuance in a state of grace—that in some places they taught one could fall and be lost, and in other places they taught he could not. And churches themselves have had angry and unprofitable controversy on this theme.

Every true interpretation of the Scriptures must harmonize with the attributes of God, the nature and condition of man and the constitution of the universe. If there is clashing along these lines, we have failed somewhere in our interpretations. If this rule had been kept in view there would have been no ground for wrangling, and the Scriptures would have been seen to be perfectly consistent. In fact, they could not have spoken otherwise than they have and been the word of God. If you change their expression you destroy their truthfulness. They must stand just as they are, and thus furnish the clearest evidence that they are from God. There are two great doctrines involved in the interpretation of the Scriptures on this point: the *sovereignty of God* and *the accountability* of man. Any true exposition must recognize these principles and give to each its proper weight. God's government over the race, you must bear in mind, is a *moral* government. This consists of motives addressed to men's hopes and fears. Those passages that are thought to teach apostacy are addressed to man's fears, and are intended to stimulate his efforts in the divine life. This *necessarily produces growth in grace*. This, now, is one side of moral government.

Those passages that recognize the sovereignty of God and the certain accomplishment of his purpose in the salvation of his people, are addressed to their hopes, and are intended to strengthen and encourage the Christian in his warfare and keep him from despair. This is the *other side* of *moral* government. Without fear, men would become reckless; without hope, despondent. The former keeps from presumption, the latter from gloom and despondency by assuring us that sovereign mercy and grace are leading us through a course of discipline to mansions in the skies. Thus we see God's plan is adapted exactly to the exigencies of the case. You must bear in mind that there can be no progress without labor and self-denial. God recognized this established order and so arranged the Scriptures—so balanced and adjusted them as to prompt to the loftiest efforts in the individual and at the same time him humble by assuring him that God is sovereign and salvation is of grace. Man is so constituted that he could not have been saved by any other method.

Now, the point of the argument is this: these forces *are so poised, so nicely adjusted, so balanced in the Scriptures, so harmonize with the nature of things, that none but infinite wisdom could have arranged them thus.* And if infinite wisdom arranged them, then the Bible is divine.

Much damage has been done to the Christian cause by hasty and inconsiderate controversy on this doctrine. Parties generally have utterly failed to define their terms and to limit their application. Hence in combating an opponent they are often found fighting a fantom. The advocates for faith emphasize it so strongly as to leave no room for good works. The advocates of good works press it so far as to exclude faith. Whereas the Scriptures assign a distinct place and office to each. Salvation is absolutely of grace, through faith as the channel of its communication; God's love being the moving cause, Christ's atoning work the meritorious cause, and the Spirit's work the efficient agent. Now, good works come in as the fruits of faith to develop, to strengthen and advance the Christian life and to show to the world the power and reality of his religion.

CHAPTER VI.

THE ADAPTATION OF THE RELIGION OF THE BIBLE TO THE WANTS OF MAN.

IT IS quite evident that any religion coming from God would be adapted to meet and satisfy all the wants of human nature and advance man's highest interest and happiness. It must have respect to man in his threefold nature of a physical, intellectual and moral being. Let us see if the religion of the Bible does not meet all these demands. To promote his physical well-being it enjoins temperance in all things, moderation in all pursuits, personal cleanliness, etc. These, physicians tell us, are the elements of health and longevity.

For his intellectual development it presents the profoundest problems for solution: the character and attributes of God; the nature, duty and destiny of man; how sins can be pardoned consistently with the divine rectitude and the honor of the divine government, and how mercy can be exercised without impairing the claims of justice. Now, it is undeniable that Christians are far in advance of all others in arts, in science, in discoveries, in progress, in statesman-

AUTHORITY OF THE BIBLE. 77

ship, in everything that blesses and adorns humanity. How will you account for this? If it is not owing to their religion, to what is it owing?

Now, for his moral and spiritual advancement it furnishes motives as high as heaven, as deep as hell, and as wide as the universe. It presents likewise in the character of the Lord Jesus Christ a *spotless example* of purity and holiness whom he is constantly exhorted to follow and imitate, with the promise of divine assistance in the hour of need and an inheritance of a blissful immortality beyond the grave.

Furthermore, a religion from heaven must make provision for the pardon of sins; for there is no fact more certain in human experience than that man needs such a scheme. This is a felt want of the race. And it must not be a mere passing by of sins, an arbitrary canceling of them; but it must be such a pardon as will alike satisfy his conscience and his judgment, and at the same time meet all the demands of a just law. This the religion of the Bible does. And this is just what no other religion, either in ancient or modern times, ever even proposed doing. Not all the learning of the earth can devise a scheme that will meet these imperative requirements. They are met nowhere else, and can be met nowhere else, except in the religion of the Lord Jesus Christ.

Again, a religion from heaven must provide for man's consolation in the hour of affliction. We live in a world of sorrow and disappointment. We are surrounded by dangers and difficulties. Notwithstanding all these changing and shifting scenes, the Bible assures us "that all things work together for good to them that love God," and "that our light affliction, which is but for a moment, worketh for us a far more exceeding and eternal weight of glory." It also tells us that our Heavenly Father is at the helm of the universe working out his plans for his own glory and the salvation of his people, and that his providence extends to all human events. What a comfort! what a consolation! to feel that we are the objects of God's fatherly care, "that his mercy endureth forever," and that his ears are open unto the prayers of his people. When the storms are beating upon us and the billows are rolling over us, I hear a voice say, "Can a mother forget the child she bore? yes, *she* may forget, yet, will *not I forget thee.*" And the response comes up from the overburdened heart, "*I know my Redeemer liveth.*" The clouds break away and the star of hope gleams in the sky, and the tempest-tossed one, cheered and assured of God's protecting care, bows in submission to his Father's will.

There is nothing so consoling as the promises of the Bible to the sorrowing and bereaved ones of earth. When the angel of death enters the household and bears our jewels away and the family circle is broken, they point us to the abode of the blessed where sorrow never comes, tears never fall, farewells are never spoken, and where the weary are forever at rest. We, too, must die. The night of death will soon close around us and "creature helps all flee," then the love of God and the radiance of the Spirit will disperse the gathering gloom and illuminate the darkness of the grave.

These facts have been verified by millions of Christians. Gentle, timid mothers, fair maidens, gray-haired sires, and little children, inspired by the love of God and sustained by the power of the Holy Spirit, have crowded the road to death and the fires of martyrdom as if they were going to a banquet. Even now I hear Christian parents whisper, O Lord, we ask not for our children, wealth, honor, or earthly glory, but the religion of Jesus, that they may live useful lives, die triumphant deaths, and live with thee forever.

A FUTURE LIFE.

Man recoils with horror from the thought of annihilation; he dreads the thought of falling into nothingness, *of ceasing to be*. If there is any question that the race has sought to know above all others it is the question of what lies beyond the grave. Now a religion that is adapted to meet the wants of man must meet and answer this question. It was asked of old, "If a man die, shall he live again?" Is there any fair and beautiful land where death never comes? Where there are no swellings of the heart, no heavings of the bosom, no choking utterances, no falling tears? In hours of pensive meditation, I look around and see on every hand evidences of death and decay. I stand by the graves of loved ones! *Oh, how loved, none but God knows.* I recall to memory their sparkling eyes, their warm and joyous words of welcome. They are gone now. They are sleeping in the cold and silent grave. The wild bird sings their mournful requiem; the dismal owl hoots their sad dirge; the wintry wind howls around their lowly bed; and the pattering rain falls upon their lonely couch. *I shall see them no more in this mortal life. Shall I meet them on the radiant shore?* I want to know. Is there a bright world beyond where the loved and lost shall meet again? I asked the golden haired sun of the skies, O thou glorious orb, dost thou know? I asked the fair and silvery moon, sailing so serenely through the deep azure of the heavens, dost thou know? I asked the glittering stars of night, can ye tell me? No response comes from sun, or moon, or stars. In my sadness, I inquired of the rolling waters of old ocean, O waters, in all your wanderings do you wash the shores of that happy land? I asked the winds that fan every sea and island, is there such a clime? Sun and moon and stars were all silent; waters and winds were all dumb.

With deep anxiety and a throbbing heart, I turned and asked philosophy. But it said, "I can not tell." I then asked every form of science and every branch of human knowledge, and their reply was, "We do not know." O my soul, is there no answer to this solemn question? Shall Egyptian darkness shroud our pathway through life? Shall we go sorrowing down to the tomb? *No*, NO, NO. I unfolded the Bible and read its holy pages. It solves the problem. It removes every doubt. It boldly declares, "*Christ hath brought life and immortality to light.*" I see the dying thief hanging upon the cross. Turning his languid eyes upon Jesus, he says, "Lord, remember me when thou comest into thy kingdom." *This day, ah, this day,* "shalt thou be with me in paradise," says the blessed Saviour. Enough, enough, I rest here. Be still, sad heart, and know that God reigns, and that there is a future eternal blessedness for those that love God and keep his commandments. And know further, that the loved ones of earth that we laid away in the cold and silent grave are only gone before and are awaiting us in our Father's house on high. *We shall see them again.*

We shall KNOW *them.* List! *methinks I hear* the melody of their voices mingling with the angels' song! Happy spirits, glorified saints! washed in the blood of the Lamb, purified, sanctified, saved, enthroned in the realms of light and life, empalaced in the mansions of heavenly beatitude. We soon shall join and help swell that mighty anthem of praise that rolls like a sea of glory through all the camps and courts and plains of heaven. O joyous hope! O glorious consummation! Without this, the universe is an enigma—dark, mysterious, inexplicable—with no star to shine upon our pathway; no light to illumine the darkness that surrounds us.

> "A few short years of exile past,
> We reach the heavenly shore,
> Where death-divided friends at last
> Shall meet to part no more."
>
> Wipe, wipe away those falling tears
> And sing to me of eternal day.

The Bible, the Bible *alone* then answers the question of a future existence. Shall we walk by its light, or shall we grope our way in darkness. For my part I accept the light and rejoice in it.

Now a religion that meets all the wants of our present condition; provides for the pardon of our sins; the purification of our nature; restoration to the divine favor; comforts us in affliction; supports us in death; and opens up to us a blessed immortality beyond the grave, must necessarily be from God. For God alone possesses a perfect knowledge of human nature and he alone could adjust a system of religion to meet all the requirements of the case.

CHAPTER VII.

HUMAN EXPERIENCE.

I WANT in this short chapter to get down close to every man's heart and conscience, and thence deduce an overwhelming argument in favor of the divine authority of the Bible.

Much has been said about Christian experience, and some have even questioned its reality. But let us look into this matter a little. It is not the Christian alone that has an experience, but the sinner likewise. The difference between the two is this: The Christian's experience reaches out farther than that of the sinner. The sinner has an experience of sin, more or less. All men have this. He feels something of its burden, its discomfort. He feels that all is not right between him and God. The Christian felt all of this before his conversion. After his conversion he felt the burden of sin removed, his fears allayed, and the love of God shed abroad in his heart. Now, if one can feel the burden of sin, can he not feel when the burden is taken away? Surely he can. Thus we have the testimony of the race to the doctrine of Christian experience. Let us go a little further in this examination.

The Scriptures divide men into two classes—those that know God and those that do not know God. The former they represent as loving God, as being regenerate persons. The latter they represent as being dead in trespasses and sins; as being unrenewed; as being in a state of nature. *These, they state, do not love God.* Now, does not every unrenewed man realize the truth of these scriptural statements in regard to his spiritual condition? *Does he not* KNOW *that he does not love God? Does he not know that he thinks of God rather with fear than love?* Does he not know that the teachings of the Scripture in reference to his state is borne out by his own consciousness? Now, I ask every regenerate man if he does not know that he loves God? He says, "Yes; I am just as conscious of it as I am that I love my wife and children." What then? Why, we have the testimony of both saint and sinner to the truth of the Scripture as to man's moral and spiritual state. God has not left himself without witnesses to the truth of his word. But he has so interwoven its principles into man's mental and moral constitution as to make man testify against himself and in favor of the truth of the Bible. Now, the point of the argument is this: How did it happen that the scriptural authors, writing nearly two thousand years ago, knew all these facts respecting human nature, and were able to delineate so clearly the characteristics of the two classes into which they divide the race? *How did they know, how could they know, unless they were divinely inspired?* And if they were divinely *inspired, then the Bible is from God.* But let us probe this matter a little further, and see if human consciousness does not bear additional testimony to the truth of the Bible. The Scriptures teach that every one must have the forgiveness of his sins. This is a primary and essential condition of salvation, which every man's *judgment and conscience approves.* Every one feels and knows that his sins must be blotted out or he can not be saved. Furthermore, the Bible teaches the doctrine of regeneration, or the impartation of a new spiritual nature to the sinner. This likewise is one of the obvious necessities of our being, for heaven is a holy place, a holy God reigns there, and holy angels worship around his throne. Therefore we must be made holy, too, in order to enjoy such holy associations. Any other supposition would destroy all the analogies of nature and the harmonies of the universe. Thus we see that the teachings of the Bible are founded in the nature of things and could not be otherwise than they are without jarring discordantly with the nature of man and the character of God.

CHAPTER VIII.

CHRISTIANITY AND INFIDELITY CONTRASTED.

IT IS an accepted principle amongst all people that "a tree is known by its fruit." Now, let us try Christianity and infidelity by this rule.

As the fruit of Christianity, look at our splendid civilization, our just laws, our magnificent government, our vast school system for the education of every child in the republic, our blind and deaf and dumb asylums, hospitals for the sick, our Sunday-school system embracing millions of children receiving instruction and moral and religious training, missionary societies for carrying the gospel to the dark and benighted regions of the earth, benevolent institutions almost without number, intended to advance the interest and happiness of the race and promote the glory of God. Look at the thousands upon thousands of *Christian men and women* who are praying and toiling and sacrificing to enlighten the minds and reclaim wanderers from the paths of rectitude—men and women that give up all the endearments of home and kindred, all the associations of friends, all the pleasures and comforts of civilization, and bidding a last farewell to the scenes of their childhood and the graves of their sires, they go forth to the dark corners of the earth among savage and ferocious tribes to teach them the way of life. I hear them sing as they bid adieu to the shores of their native land—

> "Jesus, I my cross have taken,
> All to leave, and follow thee."

What makes these people do this? Let me tell you; their hearts have been touched by a spark from the heavenly altar, their souls are all aflame with the love of God and man, and they have fixed their gaze upon the eternal throne and the starry crown. Go on brothers, go on sisters, bearing precious seed; after a while "you shall return with rejoicing, bringing your sheaves with you." Ah! what is that I see? It is a mighty host with the palms of victory. What is that I hear? It is the shout of "an innumerable multitude who have washed their robes, and made them white in the blood of the Lamb." This is the fruit of your labors.

Such are some of the fruits of Christianity.

Turn now to Infidelity. Ask for its colleges and schools. Where are they? None! Its asylums? None! Its hospitals? None! Its benevolent institutions? None! Its missionary societies for the propagation of truth? None!

AUTHORITY OF THE BIBLE.

Orphan asylums? None! What! No monuments of its march? No trophies of victory over sin? None! No torn and rent battle-flag borne aloft in the death-grapple with evil? None! Why, what has it done for the peace, elevation and happiness of the race? Nothing! If it has any fruits in this field, let them be pointed out. I ask again, where has it been and what has it done in the dreadful conflict that has ever been going on in the world against vice and immorality? Has it not, Judas-like, betrayed every interest of the race? It has carried no banner but the banner of death. It has won no victories but over the innocent. It has sung no songs but the orgies of blood and revolution. It has raised no shouts but the shouts over fallen virtue and truth. It has uttered no cries but the cries of triumph over wrecked and ruined humanity. Its history is crowned with crime. I charge it before the tribunal of earth as being the enemy of all righteousness and truth. I impeach it before high heaven as the foe of both God and man. For a confirmation of these charges read the history of the Reign of Terror in France. It has not only done no *good*, but *evil*, continually. Has it anything to offer to the sons and daughters of affliction? Nothing.

There stands the bereaved mother weeping at the grave of loved ones. Infidelity can offer no consolation. It can only say, "Weep on forever. Your children are lost to you. Beyond the tomb there is no heavenly home, no radiant shore, no happy bowers, no Father's bosom, no Savior's love, no blissful immortality. Death ends all. It is an eternal sleep." Oh, what a crushing blow to the poor, sorrowing mother. In bitterness of soul she cries, "O my children, would to God I had died with you."

But here comes the bright angel of Christianity and inquires, "Woman, why weepest thou?" She replies, "Because my children are swallowed up in death and I shall never see them more. They are lost to me forever." "Dry thy tears," says the angel, "thy children are not dead, but sleep. Beyond the narrow confines of the tomb there is a fair land, a happy home, where joy forever reigns. There flows the crystal river of life, there bloom the trees of paradise, there angels sing their everlasting songs, there seraphs and cherubims cry without ceasing, 'Holy, holy, holy, Lord God Almighty, just and true are thy ways, thou King of saints,' and millions of immortal spirits join in mighty chorus, Alleluiah! for the Lord God Omnipotent reigneth. Your children are in the happy world, where no sorrow ever comes, where no tears are ever shed, where no death is ever feared. And these bodies, though they molder back to dust, shall at God's call be raised, remolded and rendered immortal in the kingdom of God. And you, too, my sister, after a few fleeting years, shall go and join them in that heavenly world and live with them before the throne of God forever." The mother, comforted, wipes away her tears, and smiles in hopes of meeting the loved ones in heaven.

Another point of contrast is that infidelity is *destructive*, whereas Christianity is *constructive*. They are both progressive, but in opposite directions; the one downward, the other upward. The one tends to decay and death; the other to light and life. This is the necessary result from their different standpoints. Infidelity makes most of the *material*, the *selfish* and the *sensual*. Christianity makes most of the spiritual, the generous and self-denying. Consequently the one builds up and the other pulls down; the one leads to heaven and the other to hell. Another thing, if infidelity were true its advocates gain nothing by it. They are left just where they would be if they had not embraced it. If Christianity is true, we gain much every way, both in this world and in the world to come. In this world the pardon of sin, peace with God, communion with him, resignation to his will, victory over sin, triumph in death. In the future world robes, crowns, harps and everlasting bliss. Is not that a difference? Which will you take?

CHAPTER IX.

SOME OBJECTIONS CONSIDERED.

HEREDITY.

IT IS objected that the Bible teaches that the iniquities of the father are visited upon the children to the third and fourth generations. Well, is not this the fact? Is not this the order of the universe? It is not only recorded in the Bible, but it is written everywhere else. *It is the constitution of things that the conduct and environment of man passes over in its effects to another.* We are enjoying to-day the civil privileges that our forefathers poured out their blood to secure. We are enjoying to-day the spiritual blessings that Christ purchased for us. In each of these cases we are the recipients of the blessings wrought out by others. But if the principle holds good in reference to blessings, it holds equally good in reference to disadvantages.

Take a few illustrations. The transmission of disease from parents to children is a well-established fact. Consumption, for instance, running down through whole generations. Parents long addicted to drunkenness will transmit the taint to their offspring. There are whole generations of drunkards, whole generations of thieves, whole generations of murderers from this hereditary transmission. They are not necessarily and imperatively so. But inheriting a proclivity in these directions from their parents they generally become such, But nature has placed a limit to the propagation of their species, for in three or four generations they exhaust their vitality and die out.

This principle admits of almost indefinite extension and application. Family likenesses and peculiarities are so marked that if you know one of the family, you readily recognize the others.

One man by industry and economy builds up a competency, his children share the benefits; another man by dissipation and extravagance squanders a fortune, his children suffer the loss. God has in his providential arrangements thrown every possible safeguard about right doing; and presented every motive to prompt men to it, even assuring them that a contrary course long continued will shape the destiny of their children.

This is heredity; this is transmission so much talked about in these days as if it were something new. It is an old doctrine, inwrought into the very texture of things. It lies at the very foundation of the divine scheme for the salvation of the race. If by our connection with Adam we forfeit our life, it is only by our connection with Christ we can regain it.

Instead of being an objection to the Bible, it is a proof and illustration of its truth. Moses announced it thousands of years before anybody else ever thought of it. Science has finally worked itself up to this point and now stands by the side of the Bible in its promulgation. This answers the objection and vindicates the truth of the Bible.

MYSTERIOUS.

Well for once the infidel is in agreement with the Bible; for that is just what it says of itself: "Great is the *mystery* of godliness: God was manifest in the flesh, justified in the Spirit, seen of angels, preached unto the Gentiles, believed on in the world, received up into glory."—I. Tim. 3:16.

I accept the fact that it is mysterious; and from this I derive a strong argument that it is of divine origin, for we find everything *else* is mysterious. Now if there were no mystery in the Bible, it would be out of harmony with other things, and therefore could not be the word of God. But as we find mystery in nature and mystery in the Bible, whoever made the one must have made the other.

Men do not possess the knowledge of material objects around them they suppose they do.

AUTHORITY OF THE BIBLE. 95

They know absolutely nothing whatever of the *essence or inherent nature of anything.* They know just as much of Spirit as they do of matter. They know things only by their qualities and effects. A religion from heaven must in the nature of things be more or less mysterious. If there were no mystery about it, it would not be worth having.

DIFFICULTIES IN THE BIBLE.

They say there are great difficulties in the Bible. That is true. But there are much greater difficulties in infidelity. I am asked to explain and reconcile these difficulties. I will do so when they will explain the difficulties pertaining to any other department of knowledge. You should bear in mind that our knowledge is very limited. There is *nothing* perfectly understood. Millions speak the English language, yet not one of these millions perfectly understands it. But few understand even half of it. God foresaw the difficulties of our comprehending in its fulness his revelation, therefore he connected our receiving its benefits, not so much with our comprehending it, as with our *believing* it. If we must reject everything we do not fully understand, then we must reject every branch of human knowledge. As but very few articles of diet will *support* the human body, so but very little divine knowledge will *save* the soul. You don't have to *understand theology in all its vast sweep and deep intricacies* in order to be saved. Only repent of your sins, confess them before God, forsake them and believe in the Lord Jesus Christ and thou shalt be saved.

DIVERSITY OF FAITH.

They ask, "Why so great diversity of faith among Christians?" I ask why so great diversity of faith amongst infidels? They agree scarcely in anything except in their opposition to the Bible.

When they come to something like unity amongst themselves I will be ready to explain fully the cause of differences amongst ourselves.

SHORTCOMINGS OF THE OLD SAINTS.

They endeavor to make capital out of the shortcomings of notable Bible characters. Noah, they say, got drunk, Abraham prevaricated, Jacob defrauded; David committed adultery, Solomon fell into idolatry. Now, this is all true. But, now, mark you how different is this candid statement of facts from all merely human writings. There is no suppressing of anything, no glossing over, no attempt at justification, but a rigid and impartial statement of the truth. You find this in no mere human composition. You have read the biography of Washington, and it has been written by many authors. They represent him as possessing a singularly sound judgment and great self-control. This is all true. But how many of them tell you that he sometimes lost his balance and then he swore like a trooper. Why did they not tell the whole truth like the Bible? Simply because they were human and the Bible is divine.

But further, admitting the full force of the objection, what does it prove? Why, simply this, that man is fallen, ruined, and that even the best of men are not good enough by nature to be saved. It proves, just what the Bible teaches, the depravity of man and the necessity of a Savior. All too bad to save themselves, and therefore God must save them or they perish. The objection thus turns against the objector and becomes a clear proof of the inspiration of the Bible.

CONTRADICTIONS.

Why, my dear sir, did you ever examine this charge carefully? Did you ever explore the original languages? Did you ever make any allowance for possible mistranslation? Do you not know that there are innumerable verbal contradictions in everyday life and all kinds of writings, when, in point of fact, there is no real contradiction at all? I could give you a thousand. I can truly say, I *can kill* my infant child, and just as truly say, I *can not kill* my infant child. In the first statement I refer to my *physical ability*, in the second to my *moral ability*. I might say, Some men are six feet high, and just as truly say some men are not six feet high, and so on in unnumbered instances. Nobody is misled by these statements, unless he wants to be, unless he wants to pervert the truth.

The Bible is a very singular and wonderful book. It is so written that one can find the *truth if he searches for it and wants to find it. They can find the truth and be saved, or they can pervert the truth and be damned.*

It is objected that many act inconsistently and many fall away. This, so far from being an objection, is a proof of its divine origin, for Christ foretold that such would be the case. He said there should be tares and stony ground. He said that some of the early springing wheat should come to nothing, because there was no depth of earth.

The apostle likewise predicts the same thing. He says, "Now, the Spirit speaketh expressly that in the last days some shall depart from the faith, giving heed to seducing spirits and doctrines of devils." Your objection turns out, then, to furnish a strong proof of divine inspiration. Furthermore, these falls prove the imperfection of our nature and the absolute need of a Savior.

CHAPTER X.

DIFFICULTIES OF INFIDELITY.

THEY can not tell whether there is any God or not. They say they don't *know*, but hardly *think* there is.

They can give no rational or even plausible account of the creation of the world.

Ask them to account for the origin of life in this world, and they are dumbfounded.

They can give no account of the entrance of man on this sphere.

They can tell nothing of how moral evil came here.

Ask them whether man has any soul or spiritual nature and they reply, they can't tell, but don't think he has. In their estimation, he is no more than the beasts that perish. With these low views of humanity, no wonder they are not willing to make any sacrifices for its elevation and advancement.

They can not tell whether there is any difference between truth and falsehood.

They confessedly know nothing in regard to a future state.

It is a system of negations, that is, if you can call a mass of confusion a system.

It can not solve one of the great problems of existence. It furnishes no standard of right; acknowledges no lawgiver; can offer no balm to the stricken, no hope to the despairing, no Father's love, no Savior's compassion, *no home* —no bliss beyond the grave.

I ask him to account for the success of the gospel. How did it happen that twelve fishermen of Galilee, without wealth, power, learning, or eloquence, went forth against the most gigantic system of idolatry that ever enthralled the race or enslaved the mind of man—a system that was congenial to the human heart; that pandered to every indulgence; that was enthroned in the affections of the people, supported by the power of the state, the wealth of the rich, and the learning of the philosophers, and in a few years overthrew the vast fabric and planted the banner of the Cross on her ruined temples and crumbling battlements? Tell us how it was possible, without divine interposition, to have accomplished such results with such inadequate means. The success of the gospel, then, proves its divine origin.

You say, Mohammedanism was propagated more rapidly. Yes, but how? By *conquest*, by the *sword*. Moreover, it was congenial to man's corrupt passions, and promised him the gratifi-

AUTHORITY OF THE BIBLE. 101

cation of his carnal appetites. But the gospel of Christ taught the most rigid self-denial, and is contrary to the whole trend of human nature. These are world-wide differences. Besides, Mohammedanism has for ages made no progress, while Christianity is conquering the world.

Another question. I ask the infidel to point to one man, woman or child in all the teeming millions of earth whose morals have been corrupted, whose heart has been vitiated, whose life has been wrecked by following the teachings of the Bible. If there is any instance of the kind, let it be named. Again, I ask him, "Did he ever *know* of one, or ever HEAR of one, or ever READ of one who regretted being a Christian when he came to die? If he did not, what a testimony is here presented in favor of the Bible!—a testimony of human nature itself to the excellence of the Book.

Again, I ask him how he proposes to lift the burden of sin from man's heart. If he doesn't believe that burden is there, let him ask the first man he meets. Have you any remedy to offer? None! He can only say you must carry it till you sink into the grave and eternal forgetfulness.

To another question I would like to have an answer, and that is, "How did it come to pass that in the darkest night of the world's history, when the race was sunk into the lowest depths of moral debasement, there arose in Judea the grandest and purest character that ever walked the earth? Without learning, he knew all things. Without a throne or an army, he wielded all power. Amidst a moral waste around him he displayed the loftiest rectitude. He possessed a firmness that was never daunted, a heroism that never faltered, a humility that was the astonishment of the universe. Here is an enigma. I want a solution of it. Can the infidel give it? He can not. But one can be given, "He was the Son of God."

Once more. Can infidelity shed any light upon the future state of man? When death closes the scene, does eternal darkness and unconsciousness swallow us up? I want to know, every human being wants to know, whether death is an eternal sleep, or whether it is only the portal through which we enter to higher joys or sink to deeper horrors. Again infidelity is dumb. It has no voice in regard to the future.

Some speak of the Bible as if it were responsible for the entrance of sin. It had nothing whatever to do with that. Sin was here ages before the Bible was. And if you blot out the Bible you do not blot out sin. It would still rage with unwonted violence, and hell would flame as fiercely as ever. You might as well charge medicine with being the cause of disease as to hold the Bible responsible for the presence of sin. Both are remedial in their design. The one proposes healing the body, the other the soul, and restoring each to its normal state.

A FEW QUESTIONS ADDRESSED TO MR. INGERSOLL.

Mr. Ingersoll, why do you oppose the Bible? Is it because it teaches us to be honest and pay our debts? No. Is it because it teaches us to tell the truth? No. Is it because it teaches us to be order-loving and law-abiding citizens? No. Is it because it teaches husbands and wives to be affectionate and children obedient? No. Is it because it teaches us to be kind and loving to the poor and unfortunate? No. Is it because it teaches us to love our fellow-beings, and do all we can for their happiness? No. Is it because it teaches us to love and obey God? No. Then, in the name of heaven, Mr. Ingersoll, what are your objections to it? These questions sweep the whole field, cover the whole ground. Is there no objection to urge? Well, says Mr. Ingersoll, I don't like what that book says about that eternal hell over there, that bottomless pit, that lake of fire and brimstone and that never dying worm.

But, Mr. Ingersoll, was it not very kind in the writers of this book to tell you about that bad place and warn you against going there?

Was it not very good and merciful in the great God of the universe to send his Son to die for you and to make a way for you to escape that horrible doom? That world wasn't made for you, Mr. Ingersoll. It was prepared for the devil and his angels. It is true, you can go there if you want to. You know you are a great advocate for *liberty*, and you would resent it as an invasion of your personal rights if you were prevented from going there if you desired to do so. Now, God proposes letting you have your own way. You can go there and be miserable, or you can go to heaven (if it is not in your case too late) and be happy. Which will you choose? Further, Mr. Ingersoll, whatever may be your belief in regard to that world doesn't alter in the least the *facts* in the case. Hell exists whether the Bible is true or not. You do not abolish hell by doing away with the Bible. You might as well expect to blot out the sun by closing your eyes and turning your back. Let me lay down a formula: *An infinitely righteous Creator, a just and holy law*, a responsible subject under that law, with the penalty of death for disobedience and the logical and inevitable outcome is an eternal hell. There is no escaping this conclusion. To reach any other result would be to violate all the analogies of nature and all the conditions by which we are surrounded. A universe without a hell would be the same as a civil government without a prison.

You have thus far, Mr. Ingersoll, urged nothing of any force whatever against the Bible.

Now, I ask, why it is, then, you are going about over the country lecturing to weak men and silly women against this book? I have read some paragraphs from your lectures, and there was nothing true and commendable in them but what you got from the Bible. You have dressed yourself out in borrowed plumes. You have plagiarized from the Holy Book. You are getting to be an old man and will soon lie down in the grave. Is it not time to repent of your sins and quit your folly? Ah, sir, you have nothing to allay the stings of an accusing conscience, nothing to comfort in the hour of affliction, nothing to support amid death's gathering gloom. Farewell! You accept Agnosticism; I accept the Bible and Jesus Christ. Let us see how we shall come out.

SOME OTHER QUESTIONS.

It is sometimes asked why Christ did not furnish more ample and convincing proofs of his divinity. He furnished all that could be asked. To have offered more would have destroyed the freedom of choice and forced conviction. He was the subject of prophecies almost without number. There were types setting him forth in all his offices of Prophet, Priest and King.

The purity of his life, the sublimity of his doctrines, the grandeur of his death and the glory of his resurrection and ascension sufficiently testify his divinity.

Why does not God write his name all over the heavens? He has done it. Not in human language, that not one in a thousand could read, but in the sun and moon and stars which all can understand.

Why does not one come back from the dead and reveal to us the dread secrets that lie beyond the tomb? One did come back from the dead, Jesus Christ, and has told us what is on the other side of the grave, and we have it recorded in the Bible.

Why does not God speak in an audible voice from heaven? He did it often, and on one occasion some said it thundered, and others said an angel spake to him.

That a voice from heaven would not reach and affect men is evident from the fact that while God was speaking to Moses on the Mount the multitude were down at the foot making a golden calf to lead them back into Egypt.

You are still incredulous, and ask for a miracle. Well, will you accept the Bible if I point you to a miracle right before your eyes? A miracle of two thousand years' continuance. If so, look at the preservation of the Jews. Suppose the Mississippi, pouring its stream into the Gulf, were to travel for two thousand years through the waters of the ocean, still preserving its identity, you would say that was a wondrous miracle. And sure it would be. But it would be no greater than the wanderings of the Jews through the nations of the earth and still preserving their identity. Well did Abraham say to the rich man, "If they believe not Moses and the prophets, neither would they believe if one should rise from the dead." Ah, my dear sir, it is not the want of evidence that makes people reject the Bible, but a bad heart.

WHY GOD PERMITTED SIN TO ENTER INTO THE WORLD.

This is a question so profound that it would be presumptuous in me to attempt its solution. It may not, however, be out of place to make a few suggestions that may throw some light upon it. God reveals his *power* and his *wisdom* in the works of creation, but these are only two attributes of his character, and give only a very limited view of his nature. His *moral* attributes of love, justice, mercy, holiness and truth are not brought into view by these works. Hence, to make known these attributes a different system had to be adopted. That system was the creation of rational and intelligent beings, made upright and capable of standing, but free to fall. God's service must be a *free* service, a heart service. In the exercise of this freedom man fell, and thus introduced sin and death into the world. God was in no wise responsible for this result. He might have given a different constitution to things, but if he had he never could have manifested his character to his subjects.

For illustration, let us take the attribute of holiness, or absolute purity from all defilement. How will God reveal this characteristic to his creatures? Evidently it could not be done in any other way than by object lessons—*the very method set forth in the Mosaic Institutions*. Moral principles and abstract ideas could not have been communicated in any other manner. Ideas themselves had first to be originated, then *words* to express those ideas. Now, what possible conception could man have had of the attribute of *holiness* without contrasting it with *sin* or impurity? Hence all those *washings* and purifications required in the Levitical economy was to originate the idea of purity, and the inference was irresistible that the being that required in his worship so much purification was himself pure or holy. Hence they got this idea of holiness as one of God's attributes, and therefore if God is holy his worshippers must be holy also. Take any people who have not this idea already

AUTHORITY OF THE BIBLE.

in their minds, and who have no word in their language to express it, it will be impossible to convey this idea by any other means than that which is set forth in the books of Moses.

What could man have ever known of the attribute of *mercy* unless he felt the need of it? And this he could never do unless he first felt himself a *condemned sinner*.

What could he have ever known of *God's love* unless he had *sinned* and fallen under the condemnation of God's law?

What could he ever have known of God's justice if he had not violated God's law and seen the vindication of the law by the obedience and death of the Lord Jesus Christ?

Thus we see the presence of sin in the world is an important factor in bringing to our minds a knowledge of God. In fact, we never could have known the *moral* attributes of God if there had been no sin. In the fall of the angels we see only stern and inflexible justice. In the fall of man other characteristics of the divine nature are brought out, namely, love, mercy, truth, holiness, etc.

The system of the universe is not a system of inflexible natural law as taught by philosophers and commonly received by theologians. Such would be fatality.

The system is the reign of law modified in its effects by other laws, and man has this power of modification. Without this power he would always have been the slave of those laws and never could have achieved his dominion over the world which God gave him. With this power he will carry forward the conquest until he gains a complete victory. Take a few illustrations: One leaping from a tall house upon a stone pavement would be crushed. But by taking a parachute in his hands and retarding his descent he can land upon the pavement safely. Gravity is not destroyed by this arrangement, but it is modified. Or, by interposing the law of elasticity, and alighting on beds of feathers, the same end can be reached.

One receives a severe cut in the flesh, inflammation is set up, gangrene follows and death ensues as the result of the wound. The physician comes, applies the constringing powers of cold and thus counteracts the expansive power of heat, and the patient recovers.

Gold is locked up in the hard quartz. The law of cohesion holding the quartz together must be overcome before the gold can be secured. This is done by percussion, or the application of external force.

The whole department of medicine consists in a large measure of counteracting the laws of diseased action by setting up the laws of healthy action. Machinery is driven by the expansive force of steam, but the engineer can arrest this law by the introduction of other natural laws.

It is strange that infidels have dwelt with so much emphasis upon the domination of natural law and its inexorable reign. But it is stranger still that Christians have not seen the utter fallacy of the assumption and exposed it. It is not at all improbable that man will ultimately be able not only to modify all natural law, but practically to annul them for the time.

TYPES OF CHRIST.

There were in the Old Testament a great many types of Christ. Of these, Moses was a very conspicuous one. Let us trace out some of the remarkable correspondences in their character and history.

Moses was born of lowly parents.
Christ was born of lowly parents.

When Moses was born there was an edict to destroy all the male children.

When Christ was born there was a great slaughter of male children.

Moses was noted for faith and humility.
Christ was noted for faith and humility.

Moses was distinguished for zeal and faithfulness.
Christ was distinguished for zeal and faithfulness.

Moses in infancy was exposed to persecution.
Christ in infancy was exposed to persecution.

The Israelites knew not Moses and considered him an impostor.

The Jews knew not Christ and considered him an impostor.

Moses was a mediator between God and the people.

Christ was a mediator between God and the sinner.

Moses was a supreme legislator.
Christ was a supreme legislator.

Moses was a prophet.
Christ was a prophet.

Moses chose seventy elders.
Christ chose seventy disciples.

Moses chose twelve men to spy out the land.
Christ chose twelve disciples to preach the gospel.

Moses fasted forty days and nights.
Christ fasted forty days and nights.

The Israelites could not enter Canaan till Moses' death.

Sinners can enter heaven only on the merits of Christ's death.

Abraham was a type of Christ as to obedience.

Isaac was a type of Christ as to his birth—it being out of the ordinary course of nature, as being an only son; likewise *typified* the *death* of Christ, carried the wood for his sacrifice as Christ carried the cross for his crucifixion.

Joshua was a type of Christ as conqueror of the heathen.

Christ, as the conqueror of sin and Satan.

Solomon, of the majesty and glory and peaceful reign of Christ.

Melchizedek was a type of Christ as to the mystery of his person. Much useless speculation has been indulged in in regard to his character. Just accept what the "Book" says about him and there rest. He was *king of Salem*—without father, without mother, so far as the *divine record goes*, that is, nothing is said *of his parentage*. Without this obscurity he would not have been a suitable type of Christ, who was without father as to his human nature and without mother as to his divine nature.

We might give almost unnumbered instances besides these of those strange and wonderful coincidences between the characters of the Old Testament and that of Christ. A whole volume might be written upon it without exhausting it. But we have neither the time nor the space. These are amply sufficient to show that we can not account for these correspondences without admitting the inspiration of the Bible and the divinity of Christ.

I will only add a few more, taken at random.

Genesis opens with paradise and the tree of life; Revelation closes with paradise and the tree of life.

The law was given on a Mount; Christ expounded the laws of his kingdom on a Mount.

Three thousand slain on the giving of the law.

Three thousand saved at the preaching of the gospel at Pentecost.

Three raised from the dead in Old Testament history.

Three raised from the dead by Christ during his ministry.

The sprinkling of the blood of the paschal lamb secured the Israelites from the sword of the destroying angel.

The sprinkling of the blood of Christ saves the sinner from death and hell.

There were *seventy* elders of the people of Israel.

Christ sent forth *seventy* disciples.

There were *twelve* sons of Jacob.

There were *twelve* apostles.

Moses was *forty* days on the Mount.

Christ was *forty* days with his disciples after his resurrection.

Jordan, which pours its rapid waters into the Dead sea, typifies sin and death.

Canaan, the beautiful and glorious land, typifies heaven.

Egypt typifies the slavery, misery and degradation of sin.

AUTHORITY OF THE BIBLE. 115

The journey through the wilderness typifies the journey of God's people from earth to glory.

THE CONTRAST.

Rev. 14:13. And I heard a voice from heaven saying unto me, Write, Blessed are the dead which die in the Lord from henceforth: Yea, saith the Spirit, that they may rest from their labors; and their works do follow them.

All human actions are prospective in their influence; never retrospective. They go ahead of man and prepare the way before him. The actions of to-day can not possibly alter the state of things yesterday, but they influence the condition of things to-morrow, next week, next year, and on through life and eternity. What a fearful thought! When man dies, he outstrips his actions and goes on into the eternal world and there waits until his actions work out their legitimate results, and then they follow and meet him at the judgment bar, when God assigns him his exact position in heaven or hell, according to his works. *Saved by grace, but rewarded according to his works.*

In illustration and confirmation of the text above, I deem it not inappropriate to present a few cases of the departure of Christians from earth to glory:

I will begin with that of Paul, the illustrious Apostle; a man highly educated, of lofty talents, burning zeal, fiery eloquence and impetuous character. Stricken down on the road to Damascus by a light above the brightness of the sun and a voice from heaven, he joins the Christian ranks and immediately preaches in the synagogues the doctrines of the cross. He threw his whole soul into the great work of preaching the faith which he once labored to destroy.

After a life of labor, toil, sacrifices and sufferings the hour comes for him to die. Is he alarmed? Does he shudder and recoil at the thoughts of death? No. Hear him, "I am now ready to be offered, and the time of my departure is at hand. I have fought a good fight, I have finished my course, I have kept the faith: henceforth there is laid up for me a crown of righteousness, which the Lord, the righteous Judge, shall give me at that day: and not to me only, but unto all them also that love his appearing." What a triumphant exit! What a glorious departure! Now look up yonder to that innumerable throng of blood-bought saints; that mighty host who have come up through great tribulation and have washed their robes and made them white in the blood of the Lamb. See you that bright glorified one wearing a jeweled crown! That is Paul.

Bishop Bedell, addressing his family just before his departure, declared: "Knowing that I must shortly put off this my tabernacle, I know

AUTHORITY OF THE BIBLE. 117

also that I have a building of God, a house not made with hands, eternal in the heavens. Therefore to me, to live is Christ, and to die is gain, which increases my desire even now, to depart and be with Christ, which is far better. I ascend to my Father and to your Father; to my God and to your God through the all-sufficient merits of Jesus Christ my Redeemer, who ever lives to make intercession for me."

During the war a soldier returned home from the army on furlough and was taken sick with flux. I was with him during his sickness. The night of his death was dark and gloomy. The family and friends were gathered around his dying bed. In the struggle between life and death, he gazed and gazed, as if he were looking into the very depths of the eternal world, then exclaiming, "Father, I have this night fought a great fight and have conquered." These were his last words, and sinking lower and lower his freed spirit winged its flight to its home in heaven.

Some years ago a beautiful little girl died in our neighborhood. Just before her departure, she reached out her little hand, as if to take hold of something, exclaiming, "O papa, *don't you see those beautiful birds? Do catch them for me.*"

There is no doubt that when the soul is pluming its wings for its everlasting flight there is a point just before severing its connection with its earthly tabernacle, that it sees the gathering angels and its eternal home. The above statement I had from the little girl's father, and there is no question as to its truthfulness.

"If the form of the human body here be not essentially the form of the one in the future world, why is it that modest, retiring saints are sometimes before their departure, and while all their senses are in a natural condition, permitted to see heavenly visitants around them, essentially human in appearance, but transcendently beautiful? I myself have been present on one such occasion, when the lady, a few hours before her death, felt somewhat distressed that her friends could not behold and enjoy with her the exceedingly beautiful and glorious angelic forms appearing around her. Her deathbed scene marked an era in my professional life, the remembrance of which has been a source of untold encouragement amid discouragements. Her last words—I am going to be forever with the Lord—were uttered in tones and accents that I never heard before, nor since, nor ever expect to hear again in this world. If what I there heard from the mortal lips of a modest, retiring, pious, dying mother be any indication of the capabilities of immortal vocal powers, it may assuredly be said: That the mind of man is utterly unable to conceive of what awaits the dying Christian?"
—*From Dr. Wm. Kent's Christian Philosophy, just from the press.*

"Hobbes, the infidel, could never bear to talk of death. His mind was haunted with tormenting reflections. If his candle went out in the night, while he was in bed, he was in misery. As he descended to the grave, he said he was about to take a leap in the dark.

"Voltaire has just returned from a feast of applause in the theater, to be laid on a bed of death, in the agonies of an upraiding conscience. The physician enters. 'Doctor,' said the apostle of infidelity, with the utmost consternation, 'I am abandoned by God and man. I will give you half of what I am worth if you will give me six months of life.' The physician told him he could not live six weeks. 'Then,' said he, 'I shall go to hell.'

"Then his conspiracy comes before him, and, alternately supplicating and blaspheming, he complains that he is abandoned by God and man and often cries out: 'O Christ! O Jesus Christ!' *Ah! he is beginning to look on Him whom he pierced!* He is drinking the cup of trembling! the foretaste of the second death. The Mareschal De Richelieu flies from the scene, declaring it 'too terrible to be sustained.' The physicians, thunderstruck, retire, declaring 'the death of the impious man to be terrible indeed.' One of them pronounces that *'the furies of Orestes could give but a faint idea of those of* VOLTAIRE.'

"Which death do you prefer dying, that of

the Christian or the infidel?"—*From McIlvaine's Lectures.*

SIZE OF THE UNIVERSE.

"The number of heavenly bodies is too vast for human comprehension. To form some idea of the largeness of this earth one may look upon the landscape from the top of an ordinary church steeple, and then bear in mind that one must view 900,000 similar landscapes to get an approximately correct idea of the size of the earth. Place 500 earths like ours side by side, yet Saturn's uttermost ring would easily inclose them. 300,000 worlds like ours could be stored away inside the sun, if it were hollow. If the human eye every hour was capable of looking upon a fresh measure of world surface 14,000 square kilometers large the eye would need 55,000 years to overlook the surface of the sun. To reach the nearest fixed star one must travel 33,000,000,000 of kilometers, and if the velocity were equal to that of a cannon ball, it would require 5,000,000 years to travel the distance. On a clear night an ordinary eye can discover about 1,000 stars in the northern hemisphere, most of which send their light from distances which we can not measure. Round these 1,000 stars circle 50,000 other stars of various sizes. Besides single stars we know of systems of stars moving round one another. Still we are but a

AUTHORITY OF THE BIBLE. 121

short way into space as yet! Outside our limits of vision and imagination there are no doubt still larger spaces. The milky way holds probably at least 20,191,000 stars, and as each is a sun, we presume it is encircled by at least fifty planets. Counting up these figures, we arrive at the magnitude of 1,000,955,000 stars. A thousand million of stars! Who can comprehend it? Still this is only a part of the universe. The modern telescopes have discovered more and similar milky ways still farther away. We know of some 6,000 nebulæ which represent milky ways like ours. Let us count 2,000 of them as being of the size of our milky way, then 2,000 by 20,191,000 equals 40,382,000,000 suns, or 2,019,100,000,000 heavenly bodies.—*From Dr. Kent's Substantial Christian Philosophy.*

Once on a time it is said a mighty angel flying at the rate of 100,000 miles an hour set out upon a tour of exploration of the universe. He was to make regular reports of his progress. Sailing upon level wing he passed suns and stars and systems of worlds, flying onward and onward and onward for tens of thousands of years. Finding no end in that direction, he plunges down through space millions and billions of miles. No end in that direction! He now mounts and sours, passing blazing suns, flaming stars, fiery comets, flashing meteors, worlds circling round worlds, system round system, below, above, orbits crossing orbit at every angle, all moving and gleaming and glowing without impinging one upon another. Millions of years that angel has been soaring and towering amidst illimitable space and boundless creation and has not yet reached the limits of space and creation.

Such is the infinite empire of Jehovah, the Father of our Lord Jesus Christ, *"who so loved the world, as to give his only begotten Son, that whosoever believeth on him should not perish, but have everlasting life."*

Such is the God of the Bible—a loving Father, a compassionate Savior, an ever living and ever present God.

This Sovereign Ruler of the Universe offers to every penitent sinner peace and pardon and a blissful immortality beyond the grave upon the acceptance of his Son, Jesus Christ, as his Savior.

Have you done this? Will you do it? Will you be freed from sin? Will you be washed and purified, and sanctified, and made whiter than snow? Will you have peace with God and have the love of God shed abroad in your hearts by the Holy Ghost, and, dying, have a home in heaven beyond the precincts of time and the blight of death.

Time hastens—the grave is opening beneath your feet—the resurrection morn is coming—the judgment is approaching—are you prepared

AUTHORITY OF THE BIBLE.

to meet these solemn realities? If not, why not? God is calling you to repentance—ministers are preaching—Christians are praying—the Holy Spirit is wooing—angels are looking on with holy interest. Will you neglect this great salvation? Behold, now is the accepted time. Behold, now is the day of salvation!

SUMMARY.

I have shown the existence of God from the religious feeling with which man is endowed; from the universal sense of sin, which necessarily implies a law and a lawgiver; the works of creation, their beauty, harmony and design, manifesting infinite power and intelligence; from the deepest intuitions of reason and the human heart; from man's moral and spiritual nature; from conscience, which recognizes a difference between the moral qualities of actions; from the presence of life in this world, it being admitted on all hands that life can be derived only from pre-existent life.

It is proven that the abundant provisions everywhere made for man's comfort and happiness show God to be a benevolent being—that this benevolence would prompt him to make a revelation of himself to man and unfold to him a knowledge of his origin, duty and destiny; that in the book known amongst us as the Bible we have this revelation, in that it gives to us a rational and consistent account of the creation of the world, unfolds to us everything pertaining to our interest and happiness, and is in every respect worthy of God. It meets and answers all the great problems, such as the beginning of things; the origin of life; the entrance of man on this sphere; how sin entered this beautiful world; how death came; the curse of labor, and the unfolding of a future and eternal state. All these questions have engaged the attention and called forth the inquiries of the mightiest minds through all ages. But it was all in vain. They never found any solution of them. The Bible alone meets and answers them.

We have presented in this book the origin and history of the Israelites, the strangest and most wonderful people that ever lived. We have an account of Moses, their great leader and deliverer, and the mighty miracles he wrought in Egypt—miracles performed in the presence of friend and foe; miracles the most public and palpable, witnessed by millions of spectators, of such a nature as to absolutely preclude the possibility of delusion. The miracles being established, proves beyond peradventure the divine mission of Moses, and the interposition of God in their behalf.

In confirmation of these wonderful events we presented the fact that memorial institutions, such as the Passover, were set up at the time of their occurrence and have been continued down to the present time. It is shown further that the religious burdens imposed by the Mosaic economy were so great that no people would have submitted to them unless they were satisfied that they were the commands of God—that no human legislator, without divine sanction, would have forbid the sowing of the land every seventh year, from the fact that such an enactment, without God's providential care, would have resulted in famine.

The moral law is shown to have been of divine origin, because it is perfect and sweeps the whole field of duty both to God and man, and human wisdom has never been able to suggest any amendment.

Additional proof was adduced from prophecy and its exact fulfillment.

We establish the divinity of Christ from the promises and prophecies respecting his coming, the lofty purity of his character, his marvellous wisdom, his infinite power, and his tender compassion—his divinity being established necessarily establishes the divine origin and authority of the Bible. Other proofs of his divinity were presented in the various types respecting his character and works—such as the Passover lamb, the brazen serpent, the smitten rock, etc.; the fact that he voluntarily died for his enemies, the only instance of the kind on record; his parables, which have no parallel in history, and all the world can not write one such to-day; his resurrection the *crowning* proof. Further proof was presented in the testimony of angels, that of the Father, the Holy Spirit, Pilate's wife, the Centurion, Judas, demons, the convulsions of nature at his crucifixion, his prophecy respecting the destruction of Jerusalem.

By another and independent line of argument I show that all the great doctrines of the Scriptures are interwoven into the whole fabric and constitution of things, and are accepted by the whole race.

An additional proof was presented in the adaptation of the Christian religion to the wants of man, providing for the pardon of his sins, the purification of his nature, the elevation of his affections, his comfort in sickness and his support in death.

Again, an original and overwhelming evidence is derived from every man's experience, whether he be saint or sinner. He is made to testify against himself and in favor of the divine authority of the Bible.

Christianity and infidelity contrasted—both progressive, but in opposite directions, one going downward, the other upward; one leading to hell and misery, the other to heaven and happiness.

Some objections answered and turned into *proofs* of the inspiration of the Bible.

Difficulties of Infidelity shown to be insurmountable.

Mr. Ingersoll plied with questions and pressed to give a single solid objection to the Bible—which he fails to do.

The system of the universe not a system of inflexible natural law, as commonly taught, but a system of law modified by other laws, and man has this power of modification.

www.ingramcontent.com/pod-product-compliance
Lightning Source LLC
Chambersburg PA
CBHW020120170426
43199CB00009B/575